PART 2

Home Garden Vegetables

Fred S. Witte

Planning Your Vegetable Garden—
Plots, Pyramids, and Planters

by George and Katy Abraham

If you are fortunate enough to have plenty of space for a garden, you can have a traditional type with enough space between rows to run a garden tractor.

Before you plant your garden, do some planning. Most people make their garden too big and by late summer it may be a weed patch. For the conventional garden with ample space to use a garden tractor, a plot of 50 feet by 50 feet is enough for a family of 4. With 5 or more members in households who plan on doing freezing and canning, a space of 50 feet by 100 feet is not unreasonable.

However, if you plan to use muscle power, a hand cultivator and a hoe, plus some plastic mulch to keep weeds down, you can put rows only half as far apart and make your garden half the size. With this much space you not only can grow lettuce, tomatoes, radishes, beets, carrots, onions, snap beans and chard, but you also can raise bush squash (both summer and winter) and some corn as well.

Corn needs to be planted so that you have at least two rows side by side (varieties must mature at the same time) for cross pollination. It is actually preferable to plant four rows together. The rows do not need to be long ones but can be arranged in blocks to aid cross pollination. Remember it is the seed which you eat—if there is no pollination you get no corn.

If space is limited, it is best to cut out corn, squash and pumpkins, although a few bush squash do very well in small spaces and even in containers.

Mini Gardening Is Easy

As the United States moves into its third century, we find the American gardener is no longer limited to conventional straight rows and regulated distances in which to raise vegetables. Indeed, the method of culture is limited only by the imagination. This makes it possible for the urban gardener—like his country cousin—to have the satisfaction of raising juicy tomatoes, snappy green beans and pungent radishes.

What's wrong with a window box or a balcony planter with a few flowers in front for show, and beans, carrots, onions, lettuce or radishes in back for food? Many gardeners are doing just that. An incredible amount of vegetables can be grown in small spaces with a little extra plant food and a good supply of ingenuity. Tomatoes, eggplants and vine crops add color to foundation plantings.

Cucumbers and melons can be trained up railings, trellises and fences. One cucumber vine will do very well in one cubic foot of soil if it is fed once every two weeks with a liquid plant food, or if a slow release plant food is added at the time of planting.

Even though the gardener has no patch of ground he should not be deterred. Container-grown vegetables are just as tasty. Some containers that make good mini-gardens are waste paper cans, half barrels, square boxes, cement blocks (set so openings face the sky), and pails.

We have tried galvanized water tanks, cut in half, an eave trough,

George and Katy Abraham of Naples, N.Y., do a column, The Green Thumb, for 126 newspapers. They also broadcast regularly over TV and radio, and have written seven books on horticultural topics.

bushel baskets and beverage boxes. You can make or buy tower gardens (called vertical gardens) made of 2-inch by 4-inch mesh wire fencing rolled in a circle and lined with sisal craft paper, into which has been poured one of the soilless mixes. Openings are cut in the paper, and seeds or plants inserted at appropriate intervals. You can also buy or construct pyramid gardens using metal, wood or plastic. If you have a sloping piece of property, you can build a terrace garden using the same principle.

Vegetables grow faster in the warmth reflected from walks, drives and concrete pads. If plants are growing in containers, drainage holes provide places for evaporation and you will have to water the containers more often when they are setting on concrete or blacktop.

Even though drainage holes aid in evaporation, containers must be well drained. Heavy rains can cause water to stand around roots. No vegetables do well in waterlogged soil. It is better to have a well drained container that must be watered oftener than one that holds water and shuts out air to the roots.

Fresh vegetable lovers who have patches of ground available with hard packed cement-like soil can grow their produce in raised beds framed with 1-inch by 6-inch boards. They then can make their own soil mix to fill the beds. The raised beds can be any size, but the most convenient are those easily reached from all sides. A 4-foot square is one we find handy.

Used car tires make dandy small circular beds. In fact, when you have a slope the tires can be pegged in place with stakes, filled with soil and used to grow any number of small crops.

If the sun touches any of your garden spots for only a short time during the day, there's a solution. The trick is to resort to aluminum foil or chrome reflectors or mirrors. White houses reflect light, as do white gravel mulches. An equivalent of six hours of sun a day (whether reflected or direct) is adequate to grow most crops if the light intensity remains high. Vegetable beds should not be shaded by tall trees or high buildings. We've had peppers, tomatoes and lettuce produce with only three hours of sun and good reflected light the rest of the day. You can also put your containers on wheels and move them with the sun.

Left, bags, baskets, and buckets can become minigardens. Right, limited space for a garden poses no real problem. The authors made this "vertical" garden by lining a wire mesh tower with sisal craft paper and filling it with soil. Growing are squash, tomatoes, peppers, onions, and lettuce, besides some flowers.

Vegetable Planting

Vegetables	Plants or seed per 100 feet	Spacing (Inches)		Number days ready for use
		Rows	Plants	
Asparagus	66 plants or 1 oz.	36–48	18	(2 years)
Beans, snap bush	½ lb.	24–36	3–4	45–60
Beans, snap pole	½ lb.	36–48	4–6	60–70
Beans, Lima bush	½ lb.	30–36	3–4	65–80
Beans, Lima pole	¼ lb.	36–48	12–18	75–85
Beets	1 oz.	15–24	2	50–60
Broccoli	* 40–50 pl. or ¼ oz.	24–36	14–24	60–80
Brussels sprouts	* 50–60 pl. or ¼ oz.	24–36	14–24	90–100
Cabbage	* 50–60 pl. or ¼ oz.	24–36	14–24	60–90
Cabbage, Chinese	* 60–70 pl. or ¼ oz.	18–30	8–12	65–70
Carrots	½ oz.	15–24	2	70–80
Cauliflower	* 50–60 pl. or ¼ oz.	24–36	14–24	70–90
Celeriac	200 pl.	18–24	4–8	120
Celery	200 pl.	30–36		125
Chard, Swiss	2 oz.	18–30	6	45–55
Collards and kale	¼ oz.	18–36	8–16	50–80
Corn, sweet	3–4 oz.	24–36	12–18	70–90
Cucumbers	½ oz.	48–72	24–48	50–70
Eggplant	⅛ oz.	24–36	18–24	80–90
Garlic (cloves)	1 lb.	15–24	2–4	140–150
Kohlrabi	½ oz.	15–24	4–6	55–75
Lettuce, head	¼ oz.	18–24	6–10	70–75
Lettuce, leaf	¼ oz.	15–18	2–3	40–50
Muskmelon (cantaloupe)	* 50 pl. or ½ oz.	60–96	24–36	85–100
Mustard	¼ oz.	15–24	6–12	30–40
Okra	2 oz.	36–42	12–24	55–65
Onions	400–600 plants or sets	15–24	3–4	80–120
Onions (seed)	1 oz.	15–24	3–4	90–120
Parsley	¼ oz.	15–24	6–8	70–90
Parsnips	½ oz.	18–30	3–4	120–170
Peas, English	1 lb.	18–36	1	55–90
Peas, southern	½ lb.	24–36	4–6	60–70
Peppers	⅛ oz.	24–36	18–24	60–90
Potatoes, Irish	6–10 lb. of seed tubers	30–36	10–15	75–100
Potatoes, sweet	75–100 pl.	36–48	12–16	100–130
Pumpkins	½ oz.	60–96	36–48	75–100
Radishes	1 oz.	14–24	1	25–40
Salsify	½ oz.	15–18	3–4	150
Soybeans	1 lb.	24–30	2	120
Spinach	1 oz.	14–24	3–4	40–60
Squash, summer	1 oz.	36–60	18–36	50–60
Squash, winter	½ oz.	60–96	24–48	85–100
Tomatoes	50 pl. or ⅛ oz.	24–48	18–36	70–90
Turnip greens	½ oz.	14–24	2–3	30
Turnip, roots	½ oz.	14–24	2–3	30–60
Watermelon	1 oz.	72–96	36–72	80–100

* Transplants

Keep Soil Moist

Keep in mind that because growing space is restricted, container-grown vegetables will need more feeding and more water than those grown in open ground. Once fruit starts to form on tomatoes, peppers, or vine crops they will need even more water, as will the vegetables growing underground. Soil should be kept moist for a good yield. Also keep in mind that vegetables such as onions and radishes will get unbearably hot tasting if they are allowed to grow dry.

True garden enthusiasts make successive sowings of salad crops such as radishes, onions and lettuce about ten days apart (if they have the space) so that when one containerful has been eaten another is already mature enough to enjoy.

Many lettuce varieties will grow all season, providing tender outer leaves constantly if the small center leaves are left to grow. Buttercrunch is a favorite.

A perennial question is how thick to plant so that a maximum crop can be harvested in the space available, wihout crowding the plants into inefficiency. The large chart gives an approximate measure for space needed by various vegetables to help the gardener determine how many plants a certain size area will accommodate. Plant breeders have developed many mini-vegetables in dwarf forms for small-space gardeners. Look for them in seed catalogs and at garden centers.

Chart for Small Space Gardeners

For those who must grow their vegetables in small spaces this chart gives the approximate number of plants a square foot of container space will accommodate. Containers should be at least eight inches deep for medium sized and small vegetables but a foot to 18 inches deep for vegetables such as tomatoes, eggplants or corn. In the case of corn a 4-foot-

square space is desirable to provide good cross pollination.

Measurements do not have to be exact and circular containers work as well as square or rectangular ones.

Vegetable	Approximate number of plants per square foot
Beans	3–4
Beets	25 [1]
Broccoli	3
Brussels sprouts	2
Cabbage	2
Carrots	100 [2]
Cauliflower	2
Chard, Swiss	9
Corn (dwarf)	4
Cucumber (standard)	1 [3]
(dwarf)	2 [3]
Dandelion	6
Eggplant	1
Endive	4
Garlic	36
Kale	4
Kohlrabi	4
Leeks	64
Lettuce (head)	4
(leaf & semi-head)	6
Muskmelon	1 [3]
Mustard greens	9
Onions (cooking)	16
(hamburger)	9
(green bunching)	100 [4]
Parsley	16
Parsnips	25
Peanuts	4 [3]
Peas	25 [3]
Peppers	4
Potatoes	1
Sweet potatoes	1
Radishes	144 [5]
Rutabaga	5
Spinach	4
Summer squash (bush)	1
Winter squash (bush)	1
Tomato (regular)	1 [3]
(dwarf)	2
Husk tomato (Physalis)	2
Watermelon (dwarf)	1 [3]

[1] Thin at 1-inch diameter for "greens" and let remainder grow.
[2] Thin every other one when "fingerlings" and let others grow.
[3] Train on trellis.
[4] Can thin to eat and let others grow into cooking onions.
[5] Thin small ones to eat and let others grow.

It's not easy to figure exactly how profitable your gardening enterprise will be but one thing is certain, it's good for your waistline and your general well-being. Few things around the home give as much satisfaction—as well as a bit of a boost to the budget—as your garden. Studies show that for the time you spend in the garden, you get a net return of $3 to $5 per hour. One State university cites figures to show that the average home garden in its State will be worth $165. The average gardener will spend around $35 on his garden, which means he will be getting around 75 cents "profit" for every $1 he spends. And he eats better to boot.

Location: The closer to the kitchen you can locate your garden plot, the better. It's mighty handy to be able to take a few steps outside and snip off a handful of herbs or lettuce.

It makes little difference which way the rows run, although running them lengthwise of the garden makes cultivation easier. If rows run east and west, plant your large crops on the north side of the garden so that they will not shade the small crops. Keep in mind that crops should get at least six hours of sunlight daily. Try not to locate the garden near trees, buildings, ridges or anything that will block out the sun.

While certain flowers have been bred to grow in shade, vegetables are sun worshipers and do not do well near trees, both because of the shade and the competition from tree roots. A hardwood tree 1½ feet in diameter at shoulder height gives off as much as 125 tons of water in a single season, robbing plants not only of sun but also of water for nearby soil.

If you must garden in semi-shade, try increasing the light intensity by installing aluminum sheets or other reflectors to accent the sun's rays, as small space gardeners often do.

Steer clear of black walnut trees. Gardens should not be planted within 30 feet of trees in the black walnut family since they produce a toxic substance called juglone through the roots. Many vegetables such as tomatoes, corn, peppers and others will become stunted, wilted or even die, when their roots come in contact with walnut roots.

Soil Texture: Sometimes a soil is heavy clay, but don't let this discourage you from planting a garden. There are ways of making it more friable (workable). Here is a simple test for soil fitness: Grab a handful of moist earth and squeeze it tightly for ten seconds. If the soil breaks in several places when dropped from a 3-foot height, it's workable. Soil that forms a mudball that will not break into pieces when the test is applied is apt to be too difficult to work in its present state.

Another way to tell if your soil has good "tilth" or working quality is to feel it with your fingers. If the soil has a nice "loamy" texture, it's great for plants. Loam (called "loom" by old timers) is simply a well balanced mixture of large, medium and small particles of sand, silt and clay.

Organic Matter

If you find you have a problem soil, the best conditioner you can get is organic matter, such as compost, peatmoss, sawdust, leaves, rotted dead weeds and plants removed in cleaning up the yard (avoid any diseased materials). Lawn clippings, wood chips, kitchen scraps, barnyard manures, and green manures—which include crops such as winter rye, buckwheat and legumes—are turned under to rot in the soil. Humus opens the clay and encourages earthworms to be more active helpers. The earthworms in a single acre of ground may pass more than 10 tons of dry earth through their bodies annually. They mix organic matter with the subsoil. They also build up topsoil and their burrows aerate the earth.

Don't add sand to a claylike soil to loosen it. The result may be a concrete-like mixture harder than the original clay. Limestone has a loosening effect on a heavy clay soil, coagulating the fine particles into larger ones, allowing air and water to pass freely. Ground limestone or dolomitic limestone can be used. Ground limestone is less expensive and is easy to apply. Dolomitic lime has 20 to 30 percent magnesium, plus 30 to 50 percent calcium, and is available in both hydrated and ground stone types. Since magnesium is another element needed for plant growth, many prefer dolomitic limestone.

Any form of lime can be used, but remember the more concentrated forms such as the hydrated or burned lime forms should be used in lesser amounts. The big problem most gardeners run into is using the 3 forms in equivalent amounts. Roughly speaking, 100 pounds of ground limestone is equal in action to about 74 pounds of hydrated lime or 56 pounds of burned lime.

Fertilizer: A good well rotted compost pile is a valuable adjunct for any gardener. We have already mentioned how it breaks up a heavy soil. It also adds nutrients to some degree but it cannot be counted on to feed vegetables all the necessary nutrients. Any balanced fertilizer with the big three (nitrogen, phosphorus, and potash) can be added to the garden in fall or spring before you plow. Many gardeners use a liquid plant food, usually applied at planting time and again two or three times during the growing season. If a regular dry fertilizer is applied for a mid-summer snack, take care that it doesn't touch the plants. It can be applied as a side dressing a few inches away so that it can be washed into the soil near the roots, but if it touches the plant in the dry state it will burn plant tissues.

Many slow release fertilizers on the market can be applied at planting time, and because of the rosin cover over each particle they will be released at intervals during the growing season.

Pesticides: Don't douse your vegetables with sprays or dusts so thickly that it takes many washings to get them clean enough to eat. Most small gardens are easily de-bugged by hand-picking each day. Vigilance is the watchword. A few minutes each day checking your vegetables will usually be all that's needed to keep out bad bugs.

Remember that only 10 percent of all bugs are bad. Our natural predators, including beneficial insects, birds, frogs and toads will eliminate most pests if we don't kill them off with sprays. However, should an infestation get the best of you, check it with the latest control methods recommended by your county Extension agent, State university, or the U.S. Department of Agriculture.

Crop Rotation: Farmers for centuries have found it good business to shift their crops around each year. Home gardeners cannot rotate their crops that easily because of limited space. But with careful planning, you can maintain a certain amount of rotation. Some diseases—such as root knot, clubroot, fusarium wilt, and cabbage yellows—will build up in the soil if one crop is planted in the same spot year after year. Another advantage of shifting crops around into different spaces is that vegetables such as peas or beans are legumes and can take nitrogen out of the air and put it into the soil.

Corn is a gross feeder and takes a large quantity of nutrients from the soil. However, you might have to compensate for this deficiency by extra feeding, since corn plantings may need to occupy the same area year after year since they might shade shorter vegetables if moved to a different location.

Radishes, cabbage, tomatoes or let-

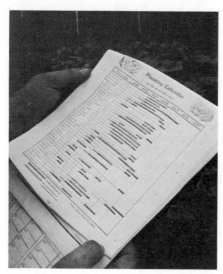

William E. Carnahan

practice succession planting. This means getting two crops from each garden row—one which can be harvested in early summer, the other in fall. Often the fall garden is more productive, and fall-grown vegetables are usually of higher canning quality than those which mature during the hot dry periods of midsummer. Take beans, for example. They mature early and are finished by early summer. The vines can be dug and that same space planted with broccoli, cauliflower, Brussels sprouts, string beans or turnips.

Summer drought and early killing frost are two factors you have to keep in mind in planting the late garden. Midsummer heat can be offset by watering and mulching. To beat Jack Frost, concentrate on hardy vegetables like spinach, chard, turnips, beets, and any of the cabbage family, plus fall crops of lettuce.

Most of these vegetables can be planted as late as early July in most areas and still produce a fair crop. Long season crops such as tomatoes, peppers, or eggplants will continue to bear until frost if well cared for. Lima beans and okra will produce a partial crop when planted as late as the first of July. Garden peas such as Wando are a dependable fall crop.

Onion sets may be planted any time during the summer for green bunching onions. Seed can be sown in spring or early summer for a fall crop. Top sets from winter onions can be planted for fall use. Those not used may be left in the row and will usually over-winter for spring use.

In many areas beets and carrots can be left in the garden all winter if a light mulch is added. Parsnips are a welcome spring delicacy but take a long growing season so should be

tuce can easily be rotated with beans and peas, alternating their locations each year.

Many disease problems can be prevented by practicing good sanitation. Plant parasites often overwinter in refuse from last year's crops. Pulling vines, stalks and overripe fruits is an effective way to control plant diseases and bacteria. If these parts of plants show any disease they should not be put on the compost pile but sealed in plastic bags and sent to the disposal.

Use Good Seed: Another way to prevent disease problems is to use treated seed or certified seed and raise your own plants. If you buy plants be sure they are from a trustworthy grower. Avoid any plants with root swellings or lumps.

Gardeners are fortunate to have plant breeders who are constantly developing disease-resistant varieties. Study the seed catalog. It lists resistant varieties and although they are sometimes a bit more expensive, they are worth it.

Succession Planting: To get the most from your garden it's smart to

Planting calendar helps in working out succession planting schedule for garden.

108

Vegetable Yields

Vegetables	Average crop expected per 100 feet	Approximate planting per person	
		Fresh	Storage, canning or freezing
Asparagus	30 lb.	10–15 plants	10–15 plants
Beans, snap bush	120 lb.	15–16 feet	15–20 feet
Beans, snap pole	150 lb.	5–6 feet	8–10 feet
Beans, Lima bush	25 lb. shelled	10–15 feet	15–20 feet
Beans, Lima pole	50 lb. shelled	5–6 feet	8–10 feet
Beets	150 lb.	5–10 feet	10–20 feet
Broccoli	100 lb.	3–5 plants	5–6 plants
Brussels sprouts	75 lb.	2–5 plants	5–8 plants
Cabbage	150 lb.	3–4 plants	5–10 plants
Cabbage, Chinese	80 heads	3–10 feet	——
Carrots	100 lb.	5–10 feet	10–15 feet
Cauliflower	100 lb.	3–5 plants	8–12 plants
Celeriac	60 lb.	5 feet	5 feet
Celery	180 stalks	10 stalks	——
Chard, Swiss	75 lb.	3–5 plants	8–12 plants
Collards and kale	100 lb.	5–10 feet	5–10 feet
Corn, sweet	10 dozen	10–15 feet	30–50 feet
Cucumbers	120 lb.	1–2 hills	3–5 hills
Eggplant	100 lb.	2–3 plants	2–3 plants
Garlic	40 lb.	——	1–5 feet
Kohlrabi	75 lb.	3–5 feet	5–10 feet
Lettuce, head	100 heads	10 feet	——
Lettuce, leaf	50 lb.	10 feet	——
Muskmelon (cantaloupe)	100 fruits	3–5 hills	——
Mustard	100 lb.	5–10 feet	10–15 feet
Okra	100 lb.	4–6 feet	6–10 feet
Onions (plants or sets)	100 lb.	3–5 feet	30–50 feet
Onions (seed)	100 lb.	3–5 feet	30–50 feet
Parsley	30 lb.	1–3 feet	1–3 feet
Parsnips	100 lb.	10 feet	10 feet
Peas, English	20 lb.	15–20 feet	40–60 feet
Peas, southern	40 lb.	10–15 feet	20–50 feet
Peppers	60 lb.	3–5 plants	3–5 plants
Potatoes, Irish	100 lb.	50–100 feet	——
Potatoes, sweet	100 lb.	5–10 plants	10–20 plants
Pumpkins	100 lb.	1–2 hills	1–2 hills
Radishes	100 bunches	3–5 feet	——
Salsify	100 lb.	5 feet	5 feet
Soybeans	20 lb.	50 feet	50 feet
Spinach	40–50 lb.	5–10 feet	10–15 feet
Squash, summer	150 lb.	2–3 hills	2–3 hills
Squash, winter	100 lb.	1–3 hills	1–3 hills
Tomatoes	100 lb.	3–5 plants	5–10 plants
Turnip greens	50–100 lb.	5–10 feet	——
Turnip, roots	50–100 lb.	5–10 feet	5–10 feet
Watermelon	40 fruits	2–4 hills	——

sown in May in most areas, then left in the garden over winter.

Mixing Crops

In our garden we prefer to mix crops rather than planting vegetables in blocks. The only exception is corn, which must be planted in blocks in order to get proper pollination. We scatter our four rows of beans between rows of lettuce, radishes, beets and onions, instead of planting all the rows side by side. Recent experiments show this cuts down on insect activity. That is the reason many people intersperse flowers in their vegetable gardens. We feel it is rather attractive to have a few plants of marigolds, nasturtiums, calendulas, or zinnias scattered among the vegetables.

Tools: Everyone needs a trowel or two, a spade fork and a hoe. You don't need a garage full of tools to produce a good garden. Small plots can be spaded by hand. Larger plots can be plowed and disked or dragged by your nearby farmer neighbor or large-scale gardener in the neighborhood.

A garden hoe is one of the best weedkillers you can get. Make sure it is sharp enough to clip off weed seedlings. Don't be in a hurry to buy power tractors or tillers until you're sure you want to do enough gardening to justify power equipment.

If you consistently plant a very large garden, a riding tractor with attachments could serve you well. When your plot is average or small a gasoline-driven, hand-operated rototiller type machine may be useful for fitting up a garden and keeping it maintained during the growing season.

If you like good exercise, a small plot is easily maintained through hoeing, hand weeding, and using a push cultivator.

A black plastic mulch can save you lots of cultivating and weeding. Don't use clear plastic because light enters it and enables weeds to grow. Place the plastic sheet flat on the ground, and fasten the edges down with soil or stones. Then make slits in the plastic. If you sow seed you can make a long slit and sow the seed directly into the row under it. You also can sow seed before laying the plastic. After plants are up a few inches, lay the plastic down lightly and cut slits or holes where the plants are so they will grow up through them.

If soil is moist when mulch is laid, plants will need little if any extra water because the moisture is trapped underneath. Sufficient water will seep in around the holes but even in very dry weather black plastic (and other mulches) hold water around roots. The plastic hastens ripening by increasing the soil temperature, and you don't have to worry about weeds, slugs or having to cultivate the plants.

Green Thumbers can turn to many sources to answer their queries about vegetable gardening: (1) Their county Extension office, (2) Current books on vegetable gardening, (3) Bulletins from the U.S. Department of Agriculture, (4) Farm and garden programs over radio and television, (5) State colleges of agriculture, and (6) Long-time gardeners in the area.

Growing Vegetable Transplants: Lights, Containers, Media, Seed

by Franklin D. Schales

Most experts on vegetable plants agree that the ideal vegetable transplant should be stocky, have good color, be disease-free, and be at the proper stage of development for best growth when set in the garden.

How can you grow such a transplant? Ideally, the best place to grow vegetable plants is in a greenhouse equipped with automatic controls for heating and ventilating. There are several kinds of hobby-size greenhouses available from commercial sources. If you prefer to build your own, plans are available from several State Agricultural Experiment Stations.

Hot beds and cold frames also are suitable for plant growing, but require more attention than greenhouses since they are not constructed to allow for automatic ventilation. Also it is more difficult to work in these structures than in a greenhouse.

It is possible—though more difficult—to grow vegetable transplants indoors if you do not have a greenhouse, hot bed, or cold frame. The best place to grow plants indoors, if you are depending on sunshine as the only source of light, would be in a large window facing south or southwest. This should be in a room where it is possible to have the night temperature no higher than 60° F. The window should not be shaded by trees or otherwise since the plants will require all the light that reaches them. High night temperatures will result in tall, soft, and spindling plants.

Cool white fluorescent lamps provide good supplementary light for plants. These are available in pre-

wired lamps and ballasts in various sizes and types. Best illumination is obtained if the lamps are spaced 2 inches apart, center to center. Since fluorescent tubes are relatively cool they may be placed close to plants without danger of burning them. An adjustable support for the lamps makes it possible to adjust lamps to differing plant heights.

If you construct a chamber for growing plants, all inside surfaces should be painted white or made of reflective materials to increase the light available.

Length of lighting each day should be controlled manually or by using a time clock. Usually 12 to 16 hours light each day is sufficient for growing plants.

Vegetables for Transplanting

Many kinds of vegetables can be satisfactorily transplanted. Usually these are classified as being either warm season or cool season vegetables, depending on tolerance to cold weather.

All the cucurbits—which include cucumber, squash, watermelon, and muskmelon—are warm season vegetables. For satisfactory results with them, plant the seed in containers that will be set in the garden without disturbing the plant's root system.

Other warm season vegetables such as pepper, eggplant, and tomato may be transplanted bare-root. However, it is also best if these are grown in a type of container that will allow transplanting with the root ball essentially intact.

Cool season vegetables include cabbage, cauliflower, brussels sprouts, broccoli, lettuce, and onion. These may be transplanted in containers or bare-root.

Franklin D. Schales is an Associate Professor of Horticulture at the University of Maryland, Salisbury.

111

Containers

Those wishing to grow vegetable transplants have a wide choice of containers to choose from. Compressed peat pellets, peat pots, plastic pots and fiber blocks are some of the types available for growing single plants in. Multi-plant containers include various size cell packs and open containers of various sizes in which more than one plant can be grown.

With most of the containers available, choose the larger sizes in the single-plant growing containers and don't crowd plants too close in the multi-plant containers. As a general rule, allow 6 to 9 square inches per plant for most vegetable transplants.

Compressed peat pellets will not allow this much space if placed against each other in the flat. However, they can be spaced further apart, and are satisfactory if the plants are set in the garden before they become too large. The space between the peat pellets should be filled with peat moss or a soilless growing medium.

If peat pots are used, when the plant is set in the garden be sure that the entire pot is buried. If the top of the pot is exposed to air and sunlight, it will act as a wick, removing moisture from around the plant roots. Sometimes it's a good idea to break the bottom out of peat pots when setting plants in the garden.

Remove plants from plastic pots or trays before putting them in the gar-

Terence O'Driscoll

Top, containers for starting plants. Left, tomato sprout emerging from a starter container.

Terence O'Driscoll

den. If the plant has a very extensive root development, with almost a solid mass of roots, you should slightly break the root ball apart, or make several shallow cuts with a knife along the edge of the root ball. This will stimulate new root development into the soil after the plants are set.

Other plant-growing containers are available such as milk cartons and clay pots, but the types previously discussed are either more readily available or have proven more satisfactory for most growers.

Regardless of the container used, it is important that it drain excess water freely. Waterlogged vegetable plants will not grow properly.

Growing Media

The materials—such as soil, sand, peat moss—that plants grow in are known as growing media.

Basic requirements of satisfactory plant growing media are that they:
• Have good water drainage
• Have adequate waterholding capacity

• Be free of harmful substances such as herbicide residue
• Be reasonable in cost and readily available
• Be free of weed seeds, insects, and diseases

Not too long ago practically all plants were grown in soil that had been improved by adding sand and peat moss. These were added to improve aeration, drainage, and water-holding capacity, since most top soil is not suitable for growing plants satisfactorily without being modified somewhat. The main reason for this is because plants are normally grown in small containers, making it necessary for the media to be in nearly perfect condition to support satisfactory plant growth and development.

Many problems are associated with making a satisfactory soil mixture. One is simply finding good topsoil to use. Even if good topsoil is avail-

Vegetable seedlings growing in peat pots.

able, it must be heated or chemically treated to kill weed seeds, insects, and disease-causing organisms. Also, if the top soil comes from a cultivated field there is the possibility of herbicide residue which might be harmful to certain plants. For example a herbicide that is registered for and safe to use on corn might leave a residue harmful to tomato plants.

For the average home gardener wishing to start vegetable plants, the best growing medium is one of the soilless mixes available commercially; or you may purchase ingredients to make a soilless mix. Ingredients for one mix are listed below. Quantities shown will make up 2 bushels of growing medium.

Sphagnum peat moss	1 bu
Horticultural vermiculite	1 bu
Ground dolomitic limestone	1 lb
Superphosphate	4 oz
Calcium nitrate	2 oz
Calcium sulfate	7 oz
Fritted trace elements (FTE 503)	1 oz
Chelated iron (Sequestrene 330 Fe)	2 g

If you live where bark from Southern yellow pine is available, the small particle sizes (half inch or smaller in diameter) may be substituted for peat moss.

Unless you have ready access to the ingredients shown, it is simpler to purchase a ready mixed medium for plant growing. In calculating your needs for a ready mixed medium, bear in mind that 1 cubic foot of medium will fill approximately 275 peat pots 2¼ inches square, 60 four-inch round pots, and 20 packs measuring approximately 5 by 8 inches by 2¾ inches deep.

Media for seed germination should be somewhat fine textured, drain well, and be free of weed seeds and diseases. Most commercially available mixes are suitable for germinating seed. However, it is important not to contaminate the plant-growing medium with dirty tools, containers, and so on when using it. The best way to avoid problems with weeds and diseases is to keep all materials used from becoming contaminated.

In most plant-growing media the nutrients added at the time of mixing may not be adequate to grow the plant to proper transplanting size. If the plant foliage color becomes yellowish green, more nutrients are probably needed. This situation may be corrected by dissolving 1 ounce (2 level tablespoons) of a water soluble fertilizer such as 20-20-20 in a gallon of water and applying this as a regular watering at 7 to 10 day intervals. Wash off with plain water any fertilizer solution that remains on the plant foliage.

Sowing Seed

Before purchasing seed, determine the best varieties for the area, as well as the quantity you need. Usually the small packet size will provide ample seed for home gardener needs.

Most vegetable seed, except warm season cucurbits, should be sown in rows pressed into the growing medium with a board which makes a flat bottom trench about a half inch wide. Enough seed should be evenly distributed in the trench to obtain about 8 to 10 plants per inch of row. Depth of covering will vary, depending on seed size. Most vegetable seed will germinate properly if planted a quarter inch deep, provided proper temperature and moisture levels are maintained.

Before planting seed, water the medium thoroughly and allow it to drain overnight. Check the medium daily after planting and water lightly if it appears to be drying out. Take care to avoid overwatering, since seeds germinate poorly or not at all in water logged media. Water very gently all seedling containers and small plants.

As soon as seedlings emerge they should be grown at a somewhat lower temperature than that required for germination. Most warm season vine crops, eggplant, and peppers should be germinated at a temperature of 80° to 90° F, whereas most other vegetable seed will germinate properly at 60° to 80°. Plant growing temperatures should be 60° night and 70° to 75° day for warm season crops. Cool season crops and tomato plants may be grown with night temperature as low as 45° to 50°.

All vegetables discussed in this section except the cucurbits may be, and usually are, sown too thick to make a satisfactory transplant unless "spotted" out into another plant-growing container. Do this when the seedlings are about 1 inch tall and while still in the cotyledon stage—that is, before the first true leaves have developed appreciably.

To spot out, first fill with moist media whatever container is being used to grow plants in, or soak com-

"Spotting" out seedlings into individual containers.

pressed peat pellets in warm water if these are to be used. The media should be moist but not waterlogged. With a round pointed object press a hole into the center of the pot as deep as the root system on the seedlings. Then carefully remove the seedlings, lifting them out with a flat wood label and gently separating them. Most of the medium they were growing in may fall off the roots. However, this should cause no problem so long as the seedling is immediately placed into the prepunched hole and the medium in the growing container pressed around the roots. Take care to avoid injuring the seedling's stem and roots. Immediately after spotting out, water the seedlings carefully.

With some transplants it is advisable to keep the plants in a shaded

area for a day before exposing them to full sun. However, no later than one day after transplanting, place the plants where they will receive maximum sunlight.

Larger seeded crops such as cucumber and muskmelon may be direct seeded into the container they will be grown in. Expanded peat pellets or peat moss pots filled with a growing medium are suitable for this. Press 2 or 3 seeds ¼ inch deep in the medium and cover with the same medium the plants are to grow in. Water, lightly with warm water and keep in a location where the daytime temperature is at least 75° F and night temperature does not go below 65°. After the seedlings emerge they may be thinned to 1 or two per pot by pinching off or very carefully pulling out excess plants. Seeds of these frost sensitive crops should not be planted more than 3 weeks before the average last frost-free date for your area.

Some general precautions to observe in planting seed include:

- Buy good seed of recommended varieties
- Plant at the proper rate and depth
- Cover seed with the same media in which seed are planted
- Do not use plain sand for germinating seed
- After an initial soaking and drain, water sparingly until seedlings become established
- Use room temperature water for all watering
- Observe safe dates for setting in the garden to determine seeding dates

Water Management

Watering properly requires practice. When the plants are small it is easy to over water. Do not have plant containers on a tray with water standing in it. If you use a tray, top water the plants until some water begins to run out the bottom of the container and stop. Do not water again until the plants show a need for water. Water of suitable quality for household use is satisfactory for watering plants.

When a soilless growing medium is used, do not be misled into thinking the plants need water if the surface of the medium looks dry. This will normally occur before the moisture level in the root zone is low enough to result in moisture stress for the plant. A better method to determine when water is needed is to squeeze a sample from the top half inch of medium between the thumb and finger. If water squeezes out easily there is adequate water. If the medium feels slightly moist but water is very difficult to squeeze out, additional watering is needed.

If the plants are where one can observe them several times daily, a good method is to water only when slight wilting occurs. When watering, apply enough to completely soak the medium to the bottom of the container.

Do not water plants with very cold water. Water temperature should be as near room temperature as possible. Applying very cold water to plants on a bright day may result in wilting, stunting of growth, and injury to leaves.

The time needed to grow a plant to suitable size for transplanting will vary with the type of vegetable and the season.

Cucurbits should be direct seeded, 2 seeds per pot in the container they will be grown in to transplanting size. Usually 3 weeks after seeding these crops will be ready to set in the garden.

The other vegetables discussed will require 5 to 7 weeks, with perhaps as long as 8 weeks from seeding to transplanting for pepper and eggplant.

The stage of development is more important than size of transplant. Tomato, pepper, and eggplant transplants should be set in the garden at late flower bud to early bloom stage. If fruits are present on the transplants, these should be removed. Otherwise development of the fruits will continue, resulting in a marked reduction in plant vigor and fruit production. Cucurbits should be transplanted when the first true leaf is 1½ to 2½ inches across.

Hardening Transplants

Some plant growers "harden off" vegetable transplants before setting them outdoors. You do this by one or more of the following: reducing growing temperature, withholding water, and increasing light intensity. Frequently this is done by placing the plants outside during favorable weather in the last 2 to 3 weeks before setting in the garden. Take the plants indoors if frost is expected. Water within a few hours after the plants start to wilt.

In no case should cucurbits be hardened. In most instances it is doubtful that hardening is needed for any properly grown vegetable transplant that is to be set in the home garden which has reasonably good protection from wind and blowing sand. It is much better to produce stocky, healthy, vigorous plants to set in the garden than to have tall, weak plants less able to withstand the rigors of growing in the garden.

Common Pests

One of the most common diseases the plant grower faces is damping off. This disease attacks germinating seeds and small seedlings, and may result in loss of an entire seed flat. The best way to combat damping off is to prevent the organisms causing it from being introduced to the plant-growing area. This may be done by using all new materials each year such as growing containers, media, etc. Also, take care in watering to prevent excessive wetness. Do not

Fred S. Witte

use any non-sterilized soil or items contaminated with soil. If you use a hose to water the plants, keep the end of it off the greenhouse floor.

Other bad news for transplants includes foliage diseases and soilborne wilt diseases that may have been introduced if you use contaminated soil. These are not likely to be a problem if you give proper attention to sanitation and selection of disease-resistant vegetable varieties.

The most common insects likely to

Plants that have been outside "hardening" and are ready for transplanting in garden.

117

be encountered are aphids, white fly, and leaf miner. Often these are present on ornamental house plants, so one means of control is to disinfest house plants before starting the vegetable plants. Also, plants brought in from other greenhouses may be infested with insects.

Control begins with prevention to the greatest extent possible. If other plants in the area are infested with insects, either remove the plants or kill the insects with an approved material. Make sure that any plants brought in from another source are free of insects.

If an infestation occurs, determine what the insect pest is and use the proper insecticide at the correct rate for control. Observe all safety precautions with insecticides. Plants growing in the house should be taken outside for treating, weather permitting.

Insect control is also important for controlling certain diseases, especially virus diseases, which may affect tomatoes, peppers, and some cucurbits. Aphids often transmit these diseases from host plants such as weeds and some house plants to susceptible vegetable crops.

The Complex Art of Planting

by Charles W. Reynolds

Before you begin to plant the garden, plan carefully which vegetables to grow, how much of each, when to plant, and where to plant them in the garden area. Choose crops your family likes, those that can be expected to do well in your area, and those for which you have adequate space. Make a sketch on paper showing the location, the amount (row length), and time to plant each crop. Group the crops according to time of planting, growth habit, and time to maturity.

Here are some points to consider in planning the garden:

—Plant perennial crops (those which live for many years) along one side of the garden where they will interfere least with preparing the rest of the garden.

—Group early quick-maturing crops together, and plant tall-growing ones to one side where they will not shade shorter crops.

—Allow adequate space between rows for the type of cultivation you will use. Rows can be closer together for hand cultivation than for use of small tractors.

—Make repeated or succession plantings of crops like snap beans and sweet corn to provide a supply over a large part of the season.

—Keep the garden producing for the whole growing season. Follow early short season crops with others planted for midseason or fall use.

—If adequate space is available, make special plantings of selected crops for canning, freezing or other storage.

Good soil preparation is essential for gardening success. Preparation may include adding organic matter, liming to correct soil acidity, fertilization, plowing or spading, and smoothing the soil by disking or raking.

Adding organic matter improves the tilth of most soils. It makes them easier to manage, as well as improving drainage of clay soils, water retention of sandy soils, and aeration of the soil. If available, add 20 to 30 bushels of barnyard manure per 1,000 square feet (poultry manure at half this rate). Or add well-rotted compost prepared at home in a compost pile from leaves, grass clippings and waste plant material from almost any source. Compost started during the summer months will be ready for use the next year.

Green Manure

Green manure or cover crops of rye or ryegrass alone or mixed with a legume will protect the soil from erosion and add organic matter when turned under.

If garden soils are acid, lime may be needed. Soil acidity is expressed as pH. A pH of 7.0 is neutral. A pH lower than 7.0 indicates acidity, a higher one alkalinity. Most vegetable crops grow best with a pH of 6.0 to 6.5, slightly acid. If the pH is 5.0, for example, lime is needed to make the soil less acid.

Soils should be tested occasionally to determine the need for lime and for fertilizer. Such tests are available to gardeners through local Agricultural Extension Agents at little or no cost. Amounts of lime and fertilizer to use are suggested depending on results of the soil test.

If needed, broadcast lime evenly over the garden area at the recommended rate and mix well with the topsoil as you prepare the soil for planting. If the soil test shows a need for magnesium, add dolomitic lime

Charles W. Reynolds is Professor of Vegetable Crops, University of Maryland, College Park.

which contains magnesium as well as calcium.

Heavy soils—those having considerable clay—may be improved physically if you plow or spade the garden in the fall and leave it rough over the winter. Alternate freezing and thawing improves the tilth, making the soil easier to manage. However, if there is danger of erosion, such as on sloping land, this may not be a good practice.

Prepare garden soils by plowing or spading to a depth of at least 6 to 8 inches. This should mix into the topsoil any organic matter added, crop residues or cover crops that are present, and the lime and fertilizer applied. Do not work soils when they are wet, especially those with considerable clay. This causes damage to the tilth or physical structure of the soil which may last for a long time. Plow, spade, or cultivate only when the soil is dry enough to crumble easily.

Fertilizing

On most soils the yield and quality of vegetables will be improved by adding commercial fertilizer even if you make generous applications of manure or other organic matter. Commercial fertilizers for gardens usually contain nitrogen, phosphorus and potash. Kinds such as 5-10-5, 5-10-10, 10-10-10, and 10-6-4 are widely used. Ammonium nitrate, ammonium sulfate, or urea may be used when only nitrogen is needed such as for side-dressed applications.

In general, leafy vegetables need large amounts of nitrogen. Pod or fruit crops respond well to phosphorus, and the root crops require more potassium. Many vegetable crops respond to as much as 40 to 50 pounds per 1,000 square feet of N-P-K fertilizer such as the grades listed above. About half of this should be broadcast and mixed into the topsoil during soil preparation before planting.

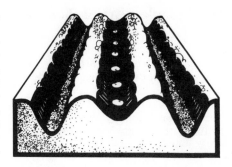

The remainder can then be applied in bands 2 or 3 inches to the side of the row at planting or as one or more sidedressings after the crop emerges.

Starter solutions are high-analysis water-soluble fertilizers mixed with water for use at transplanting. A small amount of this dilute solution around the roots of newly set plants provides readily available nutrients while the transplant is becoming established.

Use of starter solutions reduces the loss of plants following transplanting, promotes rapid early growth, and improves yields.

There are many excellent varieties or cultivars of most vegetable crops. Dozens of new ones become available each year, some of which are definite improvements over older kinds in yielding ability, quality, and disease resistance. Try some of the new ones, especially those recommended by your local Agricultural Extension Service. But continue to depend upon those that have proven suitable for your conditions in the past.

Get the best seed you can locate. Cheap seed is hardly ever a bargain. Some kinds left over from previous years may have poor germination and low vigor. If you are not sure of old seed, discard it and obtain new seed

Banding fertilizer. Place band 2 or 3 inches to each side of seed and about 1 or 2 inches deeper.

from a dependable source. Never save your own seed from hybrids; resulting plants will not be true to type.

Planting Seeds

Straight rows make the vegetable garden more attractive and easier to keep free of weeds. To have straight rows, tie a heavy string tightly between stakes at each end of the row. To band fertilizer beside the row, open furrows 2 or 3 inches on each side of the string, apply the right amount of fertilizer in the furrows, and cover with soil. Then make a shallow trench or furrow along the string with the hoe, hoe handle or other suitable tool. Make furrow at the right depth for the seed being planted. Sow seed uniformly and not too thickly by shaking out of seed packet or dropping with the fingers.

Most gardeners tend to plant too thickly. If such plantings are not thinned, plants grow tall and spindly and yield poorly.

Cover seed by raking soil into the furrow with the corner of the hoe or with a rake. Avoid pulling clods or lumps of soil into the furrow. Firm the soil over the seed furrow with the hoe or rake. Do not pack. Mark each row with a small garden stake showing what was planted.

Plant most vegetable seeds moderately shallow. Small seeded crops such as lettuce or carrots should be planted about a quarter inch deep. Larger seeds like beans or sweet corn should be about an inch deep, slightly deeper in dry weather. A good rule to follow is: plant seeds at a depth two to four times the width of the seed. Beets, Swiss chard and New Zealand spinach are exceptions; plant these shallow. The "seeds" as purchased are actually dry fruits containing several tiny true seed.

Distances between rows and between plants in the row vary widely among vegetable crops. Planting dis-

William E. Carnahan

tances are related to size of plants at maturity and to the type of cultivation to be used. Rows may be closer together for hand cultivation, wider if small tractors are to be used.

Use of seed tapes gives accurate spacing of seed within the row with no need for thinning. These are water-soluble tapes with seed of a given crop enclosed within the tape at appropriate spacings. To use these, open a furrow at the right depth, unroll the tape in the bottom of the furrow,

Spacing bean seeds evenly in furrow kept straight with tie line. Stake on either end of line can serve as marker to indicate what crop was planted and when.

121

and cover with soil. The tape disintegrates in the soil, leaving the seed accurately spaced. Seed cost is increased, but the hard work of thinning is avoided. For use in tapes, seed must have a very high germinability. Seed of several small seeded vegetables are available in seed tapes.

Planting in Hills

Seed of the vine crops—cucumbers, cantaloupes, pumpkins, squash and watermelons—are often planted in "hills". Several seeds are planted at each planting site with the sites a few feet apart. After the seedlings are up, they are thinned to two or three in each "hill". Mixing a shovelful of stable manure or compost in each hill improves growth and yield of these crops substantially. The soil at each hill may be mounded or raised somewhat or it may be left nearly level with the rest of the area.

Some vegetable crops such as broccoli, cabbage, eggplant, pepper, and tomatoes are started in hot beds or greenhouses and transplanted to the garden in order to provide earlier maturity. If plants are grown in individual pots or other containers there is little or no shock or injury from transplanting. If plants are not in individual containers, transplanting will cause less injury if plants are removed from the plant bed with a ball of soil around the roots.

Dig plants from plant bed and plant in the garden immediately. Stretch string tightly along row in well prepared soil. Open holes at proper distances with a trowel, bulb planter, or mattock. Set the transplants a little deeper than they were in plant bed. Fill soil around roots, firming slightly.

Add ½ to 1 cup of water or starter solution around each plant to moisten

A child's garden is not always of verses. Here, two young ladies lend hand at transplanting time in family garden.

Planting Chart for Vegetables

Crop	Depth to plant (inches)	Planting distances Between rows (inches)	In the row (inches)
Cool Season Crops			
Asparagus (crowns)	6–8	36–60	12–18
Beets	¼–½	15–24	2–3
Broccoli	¼–½	24–36	12–18
Brussels sprouts	¼–½	24–36	18–24
Cabbage	¼–½	24–36	12–18
Cabbage, Chinese	¼–½	18–30	8–12
Carrots	¼–½	15–30	2–3
Cauliflower	¼–½	24–36	18–24
Celery	⅛	18–36	4–6
Chard, Swiss	¼–½	18–36	6–8
Chives	½	15–24	6–8
Collards	¼–½	24–36	18–24
Cress, upland	¼–½	15–30	2–3
Endive	¼–½	18–36	12
Garlic (cloves)	1½	18–24	3
Kale	¼–½	18–36	8–12
Kohlrabi	¼–½	18–36	4–6
Leeks	½	12–30	2–3
Lettuce, heading	¼	18–30	12
Lettuce, leaf	¼	12–18	4–6
Mustard	¼–½	18–24	3–4
Onions, plants		15–24	3–4
Onions, seed	½	15–24	3–4
Onions, sets	1–2	15–24	3–4
Parsley	¼	15–24	6–8
Parsnips	½	18–30	3–4
Peas	1–2	8–24	1
Potatoes	4	30–36	12
Radishes	½	12–24	1
Rhubarb, crowns		36–48	36–48
Rutabagas	¼–½	18–30	3–4
Spinach	½	12–24	2–4
Turnips	¼–½	18–30	2–3
Warm Season Crops			
Beans, lima	1–1½	24–36	3–4
Beans, snap	1–1½	24–36	1–2
Cantaloupes	1	48–72	24–30
Cucumbers	1	48–60	12–18
Eggplant	¼	30–42	18–24
Okra	1	36–48	12–18
Peas, southern	1	24–36	4
Peppers	¼	30–42	18–24
Pumpkins	1	60–96	36–48
Spinach, New Zealand	½–1	30–42	15–18
Squash, summer	1–1½	48–60	18–24
Squash, winter	1–1½	60–96	36–48
Sweet corn	1–2	30–36	10–12
Sweet potatoes		30–36	12–15
Tomatoes	¼	36–60	18–24
Watermelons	1–1½	60–96	36–60

and settle soil around roots. After the water soaks in, rake dry soil around plants to level and cover wet area. Some gardeners may prefer to form a slight mound of soil in a ring around new transplants and add water after transplanting.

A paper cylinder wrapped around the stem extending from just below the soil to about two inches above will discourage cutworms.

Cucumbers, squash, and cantaloupes will mature earlier if grown in peat pots or other individual containers and transplanted with an intact ball of soil around the roots. They are easily injured and may not survive transplanting as bare rooted plants, however.

Set plants in late afternoon or on a cloudy day. Plants set during the heat of the day will wilt badly. Shading for a few days during hot weather helps the plant become established. To prevent cold injury to transplants in early spring, protect plants with hotcaps, plastic row covers, baskets, or other available material. Covers should be removed or opened for ventilation on bright, sunny days.

Windbreaks may improve survival

Move transplant to garden with soil ball and roots intact. After planting, cover soil ball with light layer of garden soil, forming mound around plant to hold water. Water thoroughly so moisture penetrates roots and mounded soil.

of transplants in cold weather of early spring or in summer heat. Unplowed strips of a small grain like rye give protection from cold winds and blowing sand in the spring. Short branches of trees or privet hedge stuck into the soil near rows of midsummer transplants provide shade and protection from hot drying winds.

Time of Planting

Vegetables may be divided into two large groups—warm season and cool season crops.

Warm season crops require warm weather for germination, growth, and development. They are injured or killed by freezing temperatures. They should not be planted outdoors in the spring without protection until the danger of frost is past. Those planted in summer for fall maturity should be planted early enough to mature before killing frosts in the fall.

William E Carnahan

Cool season crops grow best in relatively cool weather and may perform poorly in summer heat. They tolerate temperatures below freezing if properly hardened. They may be injured or killed, of course, by hard freezes. Cool season crops may be safely planted outdoors two to four weeks before the expected date of the last frost in spring. They continue to grow well past the earliest frost in fall, but should be started early enough to mature before hard freezes are expected.

Good gardeners plan, plant, and manage the garden to provide fresh vegetables over the whole growing season. When early crops are harvested, prepare the soil again and plant others to mature in summer or fall. Make several plantings of bush beans or sweet corn to provide a fresh supply over much of the summer. Plant broccoli, radish, turnips, kohlrabi, spinach, and other cool season crops not only in early spring but also in late summer for fall use.

Mulching

Mulches help to control weeds, regulate soil temperature, conserve moisture, and reduce soil and disease injury to fruiting vegetables such as tomatoes. Organic mulches include straw, grass clippings, wood chips and shavings, spoiled hay, etc. Black plastic, aluminum foil, and heavy Kraft paper are newer materials.

Do not add organic mulches until the soil has warmed up well and has been cultivated to control weeds, and the vegetable seeds have germinated and made several inches of growth. Earlier application keeps soil cooler and delays crop maturity.

Spread straw, hay, and leaves 3 to 4 inches deep around plants and between rows. Spread sawdust and wood chips no more than 2 inches deep.

For fall crops, organic mulches may be applied soon after planting because the soil is warm.

Organic mulching materials require nitrogen for decomposition and will compete with the crop for the available soil nitrogen. To insure sufficient nitrogen for crop growth, add a moderate amount of a complete fertilizer or a source of nitrogen only, such as ammonium nitrate, when the mulch is applied.

Black plastic mulch is unrolled over the prepared and fertilized rows in early spring. Edges of the material are fastened down, usually by covering with soil, and seed or transplants are planted through holes cut in the material. Plastic mulch tends to increase the soil temperature and results in earlier maturity of spring planted crops. It has been very beneficial when used with tomatoes, eggplants, cucumbers, cantaloupes, and summer squash.

Aluminum foil, or black plastic with a thin coating of aluminum foil, repels some kinds of insects such as aphids. By repelling aphids, it reduces damage from diseases they spread.

Mulches need not be exclusively organic. Here, black plastic is used with tomatoes. After plastic sheeting is in place, holes are made for inserting transplants. Plastic provides warmth, retains moisture, and thwarts weeds.

125

Vegetables in Containers Require Enough Sun, Space, Drainage

by Kathryn L. Arthurs

Growing vegetables in containers can be fun as well as challenging, and for those of us with little or no ground space available it provides a good alternative. All you need to grow container vegetables is enough sun and adequate space for a good-sized container.

Most types of vegetables lend themselves to container gardening. All you have to do is find the varieties that have been hybridized for container growth, or those that can be adapted to confined quarters. Some crops like corn that produce large root systems will need a very big container. Other plants with indeterminate growth habits—such as pole beans, cucumbers, and tomatoes—require a support system. Still other vegetables will grow in average-size pots or in hanging baskets.

Container-grown vegetables make few demands when it comes to location. Absolute requirements are 5 hours or more of full sun, enough space to set the container, and adequate air circulation. A nearby water supply equipped with a hose and a soaker/sprayer nozzle attachment is a real convenience, but not essential.

Once these demands are met, you can place containers anywhere—on a patio or deck, terrace, balcony, window box, garage roof, walkway. If you have no available ground space, consider growing vegetables in hanging baskets.

Drainage can be a problem in container gardening. With smaller containers, wherever possible use drip saucers to catch excess water. A large container without a saucer that sits

directly on a solid surface (a cement or brick patio, for instance) may benefit from being elevated slightly. If the container stays in contact with a solid surface, water can accumulate, causing root rot as well as possibly staining the patio surface. You can use short lengths of wood to raise the pots one or two inches off the patio.

Types of Containers

Large containers are the best for growing vegetables. As long as the plants have ample root space, you can introduce most vegetables that normally grow in the ground.

For growing vegetables, a minimum-size container is a 6-inch diameter pot with a soil depth of 8 inches. This size can sustain lettuce, herbs, peppers, radishes, and other shallow-rooted vegetables. Root crops—such as beets, carrots, radishes, and turnips —need depth and enough surface space to fill out to their mature size. Thinning these crops will be essential.

Each vegetable determines the best size and style container it needs for an adequate harvest. Very large containers are required for regular-size tomatoes, for squash, pole beans, cucumbers, and corn. Half barrels, wooden tubs, or large pressed paper containers work well.

Adequate drainage is another requirement for growing vegetables in containers. Most commercial containers come with drainage holes, but you may find these insufficient. Since most vegetables in containers need daily watering, and fast draining is crucial, consider increasing the size or number of the drainage holes or slots. Wooden containers can have new drainage holes drilled. Existing holes in clay and ceramic pots can

Kathryn L. Arthurs is a garden writer/editor for a Western publishing company. She lives in Palo Alto, Calif.

John O'Neill

be enlarged by carefully chipping away the edges, or additional ones may be drilled with a masonry bit.

If a container lacks drainage holes, you can provide a drainage layer of rocks, pebbles, or pot shards to hold any excess water until it can be used or evaporated. Since vegetables need daily watering (depending on the individual plant and your climate), the drainage layer should fill from a quarter to a third of the total container volume. Keep in mind that this drainage layer won't guarantee success; containers with ample drainage holes are best for growing vegetables.

There are many types of containers you can purchase or make yourself that can be used for growing vegetables: red clay pots, wooden containers, pressed paper pots, plastic pots, and raised beds. Each type has advantages and drawbacks. Study your individual needs carefully, then select the containers that best meet them.

The container gardener's stand-by, red clay pots, have much to recommend them. They are readily available in a wide range of sizes and shapes; they are porous, allowing excess moisture to evaporate through their sides; they "weather" well; and their weight keeps them from being top-heavy. They are attractive and blend into most garden or patio designs.

On the minus side, clay pots are breakable and expensive. Filled with damp soil, large pots will be heavy and difficult to move. Their porosity lets the potting mix dry out quickly, requiring more frequent watering.

Tubs, half barrels (originally used to age wine or whiskey), rectangular or square boxes, and hanging slatted baskets all come in wood. Redwood is probably the most commonly used type of wood, with cedar a close second. Both woods resist damage by termites and "weather" well. Wood, like clay, is porous.

Wooden containers are available in a wide variety of sizes and shapes and are relatively inexpensive. Some wooden containers will deteriorate; those that are reinforced with metal bands are sturdier than containers held together with nails or glue. Like clay pots, half barrels and large tubs will weigh a lot when planted. Check plants in wooden containers daily for water needs.

Pressed paper pots, a recent innovation in plant containers, come in many sizes, are inexpensive and lightweight. Their weight can be a disadvantage if wind is a problem or if the

Stair-step benches hold containers filled with vegetables. Sunny brick patio is ideal location.

127

vegetables grown in them are top-heavy.

Plastic is a common material used in smaller containers and hangers. Plastic pots are lightweight, inexpensive and non-porous. Most plastic containers come in green or white, colors that can be visually jarring in a garden. They are breakable.

Since plastic pots are non-porous, moisture is retained in the potting mix. This will be a problem only if drainage holes are inadequate or you tend to overwater. Plastic hanging baskets make good choices because of their weight and water retention. Hanging plants dry out more quickly than other container plants and need a firm support to hang from.

A raised bed lacks one of the basic qualifications for container gardening: it is stationary. It does, however, restrict the growing area and provide for good drainage.

A Good Potting Mix

When you garden in containers, you want a potting mix that is fast draining, yet provides enough water retention to keep the soil evenly moist in the root zone area. A mix that drains too fast won't provide enough moisture, and one that holds too much moisture may cause the roots to rot.

Most home gardeners who grow vegetables in containers find a "soilless" commercial potting mix works well. These mixes are easy to use, lightweight, fast-draining, and free from soil-borne diseases and weed seeds. Since they come in varying-sized bags, you can buy as much as you need at the time. The unused portion can be stored in its bag until you want to use it again.

If you choose to make your own mix, a good potting soil for containers consists of equal parts sharp sand (be sure to buy washed sand), good garden soil, and organic material (peat moss, leaf mold, fir bark, or sawdust). To be sure your homemade mix is free from disease and weeds, heat it in a low temperature oven for about 1½ to 2 hours. This should kill any bacteria, pests, or weed seeds present.

Other good soilless potting mixes specially formulated for container gardening are the University of California mix and the Cornell mix. Information on each mix can be obtained by writing the University of California, Division of Agricultural Sciences, Berkeley, Calif. 94720, or to Cornell University, Department of Floriculture, Ithaca, N. Y. 14853.

Some commercial mixes are extremely lightweight. These are excellent to use in hanging baskets, in very large containers that you want to move around, or where sheer weight could be a problem, such as on a balcony or in a window box. An ultra-lightweight mix also has some disadvantages. If wind is a problem in your area, top-heavy containers may topple over. Top-heavy plants, such as corn, tomatoes, and eggplants, may not get enough soil support for their root systems.

If you find your commercial potting mix isn't absorbing water (the water runs through the container rapidly and many particles float on the surface without absorbing any moisture), try using a few drops of liquid detergent in the water. The detergent acts as a wetting agent. Or you can use a commercial wetting solution. Once these stubborn mixes begin to soak up water, your problem should be solved.

A soilless commercial mix contains few if any nutrients. Vegetables grown in these mixes will need regular fertilizing with a complete fertilizer formula.

Container vegetables have needs that differ from vegetables grown in the ground. Fertilizing, watering, general maintenance, and harvesting demand close daily attention and are crucial to the plant's well-being. Vegetables in containers are at the gardener's mercy.

Planting Techniques

Most vegetables grow as well from seed as from transplanted seedlings. However, if your containers will be conspicuous (on a balcony, patio, or in a window box), planting seedlings will give you an instant display. Some vegetables, such as tomatoes, peppers, eggplants, and squash, may be difficult to grow from seed. Using seedlings will speed up their growing process.

If you plant seeds in larger containers, you can still have attractive pots while the seeds are sprouting. Plant annual or herb seedlings as a border.

Limiting the number of plants to each container is very important. Estimate the number of plants a container can sustain. Measure root crops by the space they'll occupy when fully matured. Bush squash and vine crops such as melons and cucumbers should each have a good-sized space. Corn needs cross-pollination, so plant several stalks to each container.

Beans and tomatoes with indeterminate growth habits will need supports. Beans can climb up poles or a trellis. Tomatoes can be staked or enclosed in a wire cage.

Other vegetables can be grown singly or in groups, depending on the container size and eventual size of the plant at maturity.

To plant vegetables by seed, fill the container to within 1 inch of the rim with damp potting mix, then sow seeds according to their package directions. Be sure to plant more than you want, since it's unlikely you'll get 100 per cent germination. When the seeds have sprouted and each seedling has mature leaves, thin the plants to the desired number.

To thin seedlings in a container, cut off the seedling's stem at the soil level with scissors, a knife, razor blade, or pruning shears. Pulling unwanted seedlings out may disturb or destroy surrounding root systems.

To plant vegetable seedlings, prepare the container as before. Remove the seedling carefully from its pot. (Seedlings grown in peat pots can be planted directly, pot and all. Break off the upper rim so the soil level is uniform.)

If the roots are tangled or potbound, loosen them with your fingers. Dig a small hole in the potting mix and plant the seedling. Try not to bury the plant stem or change the soil level. Tomato seedlings are an exception; you can bury tomato plants up to half the stem length as long as there are at least 2 sets of mature leaves above the soil.

To help transplanted seedlings establish themselves, use a transplant starter solution. Follow label directions.

Vining plants and vegetables, such as tomatoes, may need to be staked or trellised. Any support structure must be sturdy. Stakes, poles, and trellises should be set in place when the seedlings are little to avoid disturbing their root systems (wire cages used for tomatoes should be set up at this time too). Some vining plants, like pole beans, will attach themselves to the support. Others, like tomatoes or cucumbers, need to be tied. Use twine or plastic tape for tying; be sure not to tie stems too tightly or cut the stem. The most stable support systems are those attached to the container itself.

Watering

Watering is probably the most critical task a container gardener performs. More plants grown in containers fail from improper watering than from any other single cause. Plants given too much water may develop root rot. Vegetables that receive too little water may wilt and die.

Improper watering can also cause blossoms to drop.

Ideally, potting mix in a container should be evenly moist throughout—not waterlogged. Plants need ample moisture to prevent "water stress."

Many gardeners water containers in the morning, adding water until it comes out the drainage holes. This method is recommended only if your potting mix is fast-draining and the container has adequate drainage holes.

With watering in the morning, foliage should be dry by evening, helping prevent diseases. If you live in a hot, dry climate, check your containers again in the early afternoon. Vegetables in containers will dry out faster than those in the ground.

The best way to water container plants is by hand—either with a hose that has a sprayer attachment or a watering can. More inventive gardeners may want to try automatic watering systems, but these can be costly.

A few words of warning: Hoses without a sprayer/mister nozzle can disperse water with enough force to create holes in the potting mix. This can damage root systems. Also, if your hose sits in the sun, let enough water run through it until the water is cool or lukewarm. Hot water isn't good for plant roots.

Mulching and Fertilizing

Mulching, especially in larger containers, can help keep moisture in the soil longer. You can use any of the organic mulches, such as wood chips, compost, or sawdust, very effectively. Plastic mulches will work, but they aren't too attractive.

Vegetables grown in containers are trapped. Once they use the nutrients available in the potting mix, the root systems have nowhere else to go. Frequent and regular fertilizing is the answer.

The container gardener will find many kinds of complete fertilizers specially formulated for use on vegetables. Common N-P-K breakdowns are 18-20-16, 18-12-10, or 10-10-10. Fish emulsion is also commonly used.

These fertilizers can be applied in a liquid solution in conjunction with watering, scratched or dug in dry form into the soil surface, or, in the case of timed-release fertilizers, sprinkled on the soil surface. Whichever type you choose, follow the label directions carefully.

Since containers with vegetables should be watered daily, nutrients can leach out of the soil rapidly. Consider applying fertilizer at half strength twice as often; this should assure your vegetables consistent fertilizer.

Timed-release fertilizers are also a good solution. Their capsules are constructed to release a tiny amount of fertilizer each time the vegetable is watered, and you only apply this type once a season.

Container gardeners are fortunate since each vegetable is isolated by its pot, and no one crop is concentrated, lessening the chance of a pest infestation. Unfortunately, pests can still present a problem. Most insects, such as whiteflies and aphids, can be discouraged with blasts of water. Tomato hornworms can be hand picked. Snails and slugs can be baited with a chemical.

If pest damage becomes intolerable or your crop is being damaged, use a spray formulated to kill the damaging pest. Be sure any chemical sprays you choose are recommended for use on vegetables.

Choosing Vegetables

Vegetables that grow best in containers share certain characteristics. They will grow in confined spaces, usually have determinate growth habits, need a minimum of added support, and produce a large enough crop yield to make your efforts worthwhile.

Some vegetables, such as asparagus and corn, have such large root systems that trying to grow them in containers—if you can locate pots large enough—is very difficult. A low crop yield per plant, again asparagus and corn are good examples, is another deterrent to container culture.

Listed here are the vegetables, and specialized varieties of more difficult vegetables, that are recommended as best adapted to life in containers. Most have compact growth habits and relatively high crop yields. Some have been specifically hybridized for container growth.

Other varieties of recommended vegetables can also be adapted to containers, but because of their size or growth habits will require more work and attention. With the popularity of growing vegetables in containers on the upswing, seed hybridizers should continue to find new, more adaptable vegetable varieties.

Artichoke. "Green Globe" is a consistent producer. Use very large containers.

Beans. Use bush forms in containers for best results. Pole varieties need supports (poles in teepee shape or trellises will work); plants may also be topheavy. Snap beans to try are "Green Crop", "Tender Crop", "Bush Romano", "Bush Blue Lake", "Royalty" (purple pod). Lima bean varieties include "Henderson Bush" and "Jackson Wonder Bush".

Beets. These root crops will need at least 10 to 12 inches of soil depth and about a 3- to 4-inch space between each plant. Two good varieties are "Little Egypt" and "Early Red Ball".

Brussels sprouts. This cool weather crop needs a large container, but produces a heavy yield per plant. Two compact varieties are "Jade Cross" and "Long Island Improved".

Cabbage. Regular varieties aren't recommended for containers. You can try dwarf varieties such as "Dwarf Morden" and "Earliana". Chinese cabbage is a good container crop; plant "Michihli" or "Burpee Hybrid".

Carrots. Be sure to use containers with enough depth (at least 12 inches up to 20) for root formation and a very light mix for good growth. Any variety will grow in containers. Some of the shorter varieties are fine: try "Danvers Half Long", "Little Finger", "Short & Sweet", and "Tiny Sweet".

Chard. Any variety will grow in a large container, at least 2 feet deep. Use a potting mix with enough support for a large root system.

Collards. If you harvest the outer leaves consistently, you can have a continuous supply of greens. "Vates" is a compact variety.

Corn. Because of its size, low crop yield per plant, and need for cross pollination, corn isn't a good container vegetable. If you still want to try it, plant dwarf or midget varieties. Plant at least three stalks per container. Some varieties to consider are "Golden Midget", "Golden Cross Bantam", "Midget Hybrid", and "Fireside Popcorn".

Cucumber. Cucumbers need a large container, and some can adapt to a trellis support. The varieties that form small vines or are bushlike are best: "Little Minnie", "Tiny Dill", "Spartan Dawn", and "Cherokee 7". "Patio Pik" and "Pot Luck" were developed for containers and can be used in hanging baskets.

Eggplant. Eggplant needs a large container to grow well. Since warm soil is required for good growth, plant seedlings. Any variety will grow in containers; smaller varieties are "Morden Midget" and "Slim Jim."

Herbs. All of the herbs can be grown in containers.

Endive. Plant any variety in early spring; reseed containers again in August for a fall crop.

Kale. Plant any variety in a large container. Harvest outer leaves to extend the crop.

Kohlrabi. This vegetable's unusual appearance makes it a conversation piece in a container. Any variety is fast-growing.

Lettuce. Because lettuce is a cool weather crop, being able to move it to a shaded or protected spot is a plus. Try growing leaf lettuce in containers; harvest the outer leaves for a continuous harvest. Any variety can be container-grown.

Melons. Because of the plant size and low yield, growing melons in containers is impractical. You can try some of the midget varieties in large containers. A midget cantaloupe is "Minnesota Midget". "Yellow Lollipop", "Red Lollipop", and "Little Midget" are small-size watermelons.

Mustard Greens. Extend the harvest by picking outer leaves. Mustard greens are a good container crop.

Okra. Plant this Southern favorite in a large container. Plants have a high crop yield. Try "Dwarf Green Long Pod", "Clemson Spineless", and "Red River".

Onions. While most onions can be grown in containers, the larger types make unattractive displays. Chives and green bunching onions (scallions) are good pot plants.

Peas. Peas grown in containers demand a lot of attention, need large containers, and produce a small yield for your time and effort. If you want the challenge, you can try "Little Marvel", "Green Arrow", "Dwarf Gray Sugar", and "Mighty Midget"

Rhubarb. In larger containers, any variety will do well and make an attractive display. Move pots to a garage or sheltered area during a freeze.

Radishes. All varieties make excellent container plants. You can use them as borders in large containers.

Spinach. Another cool season crop, spinach can be grown in boxes or large containers. New Zealand spinach (not a true spinach) grows well in pots and recovers rapidly from cutting.

Squash. Not a good container crop because of its size, but you can attempt it if you use very large pots and plant bush varieties. One new hybrid, "Scallopini", forms a compact bush plant.

Tomatoes. Many varieties have been hybridized especially for containers. Use medium to large containers since most tomatoes need some support. Use stakes or a wire cage as a support; be sure the wire squares are large enough to allow for harvesting.

Some tomato varieties to try are "Tiny Tim", "Small Fry", "Patio Hybrid", "Sugar Lump", "Tumbling Tom" (recommended for hanging baskets), "Stakeless", "Burpee's Pixie", "Salad Top", "Sweet 100", and "Toy Boy".

Harvesting

Since container gardening is a small-scale operation, most crops will be harvested for a specific meal. This allows you to pick them just before meal preparation begins so they will be at their freshest.

Pick leafy crops carefully, such as chard, lettuce, or collards. Remove only the outer leaves to keep the plant producing. Root crops, such as radishes or carrots, should be pulled out without disturbing their neighbors. Crops that have fruit ripening continuously, like tomatoes and beans, should be picked so as not to ruin or destroy future fruit.

Try not to pick more of a crop than you can use. If you harvest too much, keep your vegetables in the crisper section of a refrigerator. It is unlikely that a container crop would produce enough to make canning or freezing worthwhile.

Play It Cool With Cole Crops (Cabbage, Etc.); They Attain Best Quality If Matured in Fall

by Philip A. Minges

The closely related vegetables commonly referred to as cole crops include cabbage, cauliflower, brussels sprouts, broccoli, and kohlrabi. Being frost-tolerant, they are valuable for extending the harvest season for gardens after frost or cool weather has eliminated the popular warm season vegetables.

In fact, this group of vegetables develops best quality and remains edible longer in the garden when matured during the moderately cool weather and shorter days of fall. When maturing in hot weather, the harvest period is relatively short, quality often is less desirable, and yields are likely to be lower.

The crops are adapted to all sections of the United States provided proper planting dates are selected. In areas with short growing seasons, spring plantings for summer and early fall harvest work well. In intermediate areas, early spring plantings for summer harvest are possible while summer plantings for fall harvest are ideal. In areas with mild winters, late summer or early fall plantings for fall and winter harvest are common.

For broccoli, cabbage and cauliflower, planting two or more varieties of differing maturities—for example, a fast and a slow maturing one—can easily extend the harvest season from a single planting from a week or so to a month or more.

Local information on varieties and preferred planting dates should be sought by gardeners. Poor selection of varieties and/or planting dates may lead to poor results due to premature seeding caused by undue exposure to cool temperatures early in the growing season and other problems.

As a group these vegetables rank fairly high in nutritional value and are quite adaptable for use fresh or cooked and for preserving. Cauliflower is suitable for freezing, canning or pickling. Broccoli and brussels sprouts are excellent for freezing. Cabbage when kept cool and moist will store for several weeks after harvest and, of course, it can be preserved as sauerkraut.

Cole crops can be grown on a wide range of soils. Fertile, deep, well-drained, sandy and silt loams are the most desirable. Have a soil test made; your county Extension office can tell you how to have this done. Good drainage is particularly important where the garden will be continued into or through the winter months.

A soil pH level of around 6.5 or slightly above is desirable for efficient use of fertilizer and soil nutrients, and for reducing development of a soil-borne disease called clubroot. If the soil is acid as indicated by a pH reading below 6.0, apply lime before preparing the garden. In humid areas with acid soils, apply it at a rate of 10 pounds per 100 square feet every 3 to 5 years. This should maintain a good soil pH once the pH has been brought up to the desirable level.

In some parts of the Eastern United States and generally in the Western portions, soils tend to be alkaline and therefore don't require lime. In many desert areas a problem may be excessively high pH and/or a high salt content. Avoid highly saline soils if possible, or correct them by leaching

Philip A. Minges is Professor of Vegetable Crops, Cornell University, Ithaca, N.Y.

133

—perhaps in combination with the addition of sulfur. There are a few exceptions, but minor element problems seldom are serious when the pH level is in the range of 6.0 to 7.5.

Fertile soils may supply sufficient amounts of nitrogen, phosphorus and potassium for cole crop needs, making fertilizer applications unnecessary. In the Western States nitrogen is often the only limiting nutrient, though phosphorus applications may benefit late fall and winter plantings.

In the humid Eastern States a complete fertilizer usually is advisable. On new garden sites or where fertility is known to be low, 3 to 4 pounds per 100 square feet of a 5-10-10 fertilizer is advised. On more fertile soils 1 to 1½ pounds may be adequate. A sidedressing with nitrogen at a rate of about a half pound of ammonium nitrate per 20 feet of row, applied 2 to 4 weeks after planting, may be beneficial on sandy soils, when heavy rains occurred shortly after planting, or during relatively cool weather.

Planting and Culture

Cole crops can be established in the garden either by setting transplants or by seeding. Using transplants is the rule for cabbage, broccoli, cauliflower and brussels sprouts in many areas while kohlrabi normally is seeded. Using transplants saves 2 to 3 weeks growing time in the garden. But for fall crops of cabbage, broccoli and cauliflower, direct seeding with later thinning is very satisfactory. To obtain similar maturity, seeding should be done about 2 weeks earlier than setting transplants.

A desirable transplant is 4 to 5 weeks old with 3 to 5 true leaves, and is free of diseases. Older transplants sometimes will head a bit earlier but otherwise there is little advantage; in fact, head sizes often average considerably smaller when old, large plants are set out. You can buy transplants at local garden supply outlets, or grow them at home. In direct seedings, the plants being thinned can serve as transplants if carefully dug. When reset immediately, they will reach harvest stage some 10 to 14 days later than the undisturbed plants —thus spreading the harvest period from a single seeding.

Transplants to be used for early spring planting should be grown at temperatures no lower than 60° F to lessen the hazard of premature flower stalk formation.

Either flat or bed culture is suitable. Beds have an advantage when soil drainage is likely to be slow during the late fall and winter months, and where furrow irrigation is practiced. In the Western States, beds about 6 to 8 inches high and 30 to 42 inches center to center are common. On the wider beds, 2 rows 12 to 14 inches apart can be used for most of these crops except brussels sprouts, for which 1 row is usual. Fertilizer can be broadcast before forming the beds or banded later along the sides. Forming the beds a few days ahead of planting to allow the soil to settle a bit is a good practice when time permits.

In transplanting, dig holes deep enough to accommodate the root system (or soil block), place the plant in the hole, and then firm some soil around the roots or soil block. Often it helps to apply a cup of starter solution containing some soluble fertilizer, and in areas where root maggot is troublesome a chemical for control of this pest.

After the water has drained down, pile more soil around the plant so the stem is covered a bit higher than it was in the plant-growing container.

In direct seeding, open shallow furrows and drop seeds about 1 inch apart. Partially cover the seed with soil and firm it over the seed, then finish covering with loose soil to a total of ½ to 1 inch in depth. If the soil is dry and rains are not expected, water immediately. In hot, dry weather, you may need to sprinkle or otherwise apply water a few times to insure adequate germination. When the plants show 2 to 3 true leaves, thin them to the desired spacings.

A row spacing of 30 to 36 inches is suitable. Slightly closer rows will do when space is limited, especially for kohlrabi. Common spacings in the row are 15 to 24 inches for cabbage, cauliflower, and broccoli; 30 to 36 inches for brussels sprouts; and 4 to 6 inches for kohlrabi.

You can control weeds easiest when they are small, using a hoe or small hand cultivator. Approved herbicides can be applied before planting and worked into the soil when rather large plantings are contemplated. Consult the label for rates and other instructions. Weedy gardens are never as productive as those kept weed-free.

All cole crops develop most rapidly and with best quality when adequate soil moisture is provided throughout the season. In humid areas, irrigation during dry periods can be helpful. In areas with normally dry summers, irrigation is essential until fall and winter rains begin. Light irrigation should start at transplanting or seeding and the amount gradually increased as the plants grow until about 1 to 1½ inches of water is applied weekly.

Pest Control

As a rule, fungicides and insecticides are essential for controlling certain diseases and insect pests on cole crops. For some diseases other precautions are desirable, such as use of disease-free seed or transplants and resistant varieties.

Insect pests tend to be localized but flea beetles, aphids and cabbage worms are common over the country. Flea beetles are most damaging on

young plants, so control for these comes early. Cabbage maggots which feed on the roots, causing plants to wilt prematurely during hot weather, also must be controlled at planting time. Aphids and worms usually cause trouble later in the season. Slugs or snails are a bothersome pest in many areas.

Most fungicides are non-toxic to humans and animals, and there are a number of fairly safe insecticides that give reasonable control of insect pests.

Cole crops generally are biennials or have similar tendencies. What this means is the plants can be induced to initiate seedstalks and flowers by exposure to cool temperatures over a period of several days. If that occurs early in the growing season, the crops may fail to produce a usable product.

The threshold temperatures appear to be in the range of 50° to 55° F, and the plants increase in sensitivity to the cold as they increase in size and age. Thus in areas with mild winters, plants set out too late in the fall or too early in the spring may go to

To produce high quality cabbage the gardener must control weeds, insects, and diseases.

seed prematurely. In the case of broccoli and cauliflower, crops where the developing flower stalk is the edible product, the result is a very small curd or head. The use of slow-bolting varieties coupled with proper planting dates will avoid these problems, unless the early part of the growing season is cooler than normal.

Varieties

Hybrid varieties (F_1) are available for cabbage, broccoli, cauliflower and brussels sprouts. Usually they are more uniform in plant size, maturity and size of head than standard varieties and often the total yield is greater. The uniformity of maturity may not be an advantage for the home gardener, except when the crop is grown primarily for processing.

Varieties differ in many characteristics including color, days to maturity, uniformity, yields, ease of bolting, product size, length of time the product remains usable, and resistance to diseases and disorders. Generally there are not as great differences in flavor or eating quality as among varieties of other vegetables. And most varieties in this grouping are rather widely adapted, the exceptions being the winter types of cauliflower and late varieties of broccoli which are limited to areas of mild winters.

Broccoli—The green buds and flower stems are the edible portion. The center shoot is large, ranging from 5 to 10 inches or more across depending on the variety, growing conditions and other factors. It should be harvested before the buds begin to separate or start to show yellow color. The heads remain in edible condition fairly long in cool weather, but pass prime maturity very quickly when it is hot. After the center head is cut, smaller side shoots develop which can extend the harvest season up to a month or more.

Broccoli is of best quality if consumed soon after harvest, though it

Center head of broccoli with side shoots. Shoots can prolong harvest season month or more after head is cut.

will keep a few days under high humidity and low temperatures (near 32° F).

Spartan Early, Coastal, Italian Green Sprouting, Early One and De-Cicco are among the fast growing standard varieties that are suitable for the Central and Eastern portions of the United States. Waltham 29 is a popular late one. Medium strains of Green Sprouting, Topper and Pacifica are popular on the West Coast. Early hybrids (F_1) include Green Comet, Gem, Bravo and Premium Crop. From 50 to 85 days are required from transplanting to harvest, or 65 to 110 days when seeded in the garden. Late summer and early spring plantings require more time than plantings in periods of longer days and higher temperatures.

Cabbage—Types of varieties vary in color from green with smooth or

savoyed leaves to reddish purple, and in shape from flat to pointed. The intermediate round types are the most common.

There are numerous acceptable varieties. Some Fusarium-resistant standard varieties are Resistant Golden Acre, Resistant Wakefield, Greenback, and Resistant Danish (in order of maturity from early to late). Other popular standard varieties include

Early Marvel, Golden Acre, Copenhagen Market, Early Round Dutch (slower bolting), Red Acre, Danish Ballhead and Chieftain Savoy.

Some Fusarium-resistant hybrids are Wizard, Market Victor, Gourmet, Market Prize, King Cole, and Excel. Other hybrids include Emerald Cross, Stonehead, Ruby Ball, Red Head, Savoy King, and Savoy Ace.

The heads are usable as soon as they become fairly firm. Early varieties grown under favorable conditions will reach the harvest stage 55 to 70 days after transplanting. Later varieties may require 110 to 120 days or more. In warm weather, heads may split open fairly soon after reaching the harvest stage. In cool weather they may remain good for several weeks. In cold regions, cabbage should be harvested before hard freezes occur. It can be stored at high humidity and low temperature (32—40° F) for several months.

Cabbage planted early for summer harvest often will develop small heads on the stem after the center head is removed. These are quite edible and can be used to extend the harvest period.

Cauliflower—The Snowball group of varieties is the most commonly used in home gardens. Snow King, Snow Crown and Snowflower are fast-growing hybrids. Self Blanch and Snowball Y are examples of good standard late varieties. The purple headed type, somewhat of a novelty, turns green when cooked and resembles broccoli. In southern California and probably in other warm winter areas, the winter type will perform satisfactorily. November-December, February, and Mayflower are common varieties.

The ideal time to set out cauliflower plants is late July or August,

Top, early hybrid Premium Crop broccoli. Left, Savoy cabbage.

as late September and October often provide the most desirable weather for developing good quality. Covering the developing heads helps in producing pure white curds, but the slightly yellowish curds obtained without covering are generally of equal quality. Exposed curds (heads) may be injured by frosts. So as the frosty season approaches, protect the heads by tying together the inner leaves or breaking an inner leaf or two over the head.

The heads are ready to use as soon as they reach suitable size. They should be cut before the parts begin to separate or become "ricey". As with broccoli, cauliflower tastes best soon after harvest.

Brussels Sprouts—This crop is best grown for fall harvest by setting out plants in June or early July. Catskill, Jade Cross (F_1), and Long Island Im-

proved are common varieties. In warm weather the sprouts tend to be loose and of poor quality, but they firm up and become milder in flavor as the cool weather arrives. Sprouts 1 to 1½ inches in diameter are desirable. In harvesting, remove the leaf beneath the sprout and cut or break off the sprout. Harvesting can continue as long as the sprouts develop.

Debudding, cutting out the growing point in late August or early September after the plants are 15 to 20 inches tall, tends to induce the sprouts on the plant to be ready at about the same time. This practice may be helpful in areas where winter sets in early.

Kohlrabi—Kohlrabi, a "stem turnip", can be eaten fresh or boiled or added to soups and stews. It can be planted in the spring, but usually is best for use in the fall (and winter in the South) after frost-tender vegetables are gone. Seeded in the garden, kohlrabi is ready to use in 55 to 65 days. Harvest kohlrabi when it is 2 to 4 inches in size and the flesh is still tender.

Suitable varieties include Early White Vienna and Early Purple Vienna.

Chinese Cabbage—This vegetable, though a different species than the cole crops, has similar culture. It can be used raw or cooked.

Plants tend to go to seed rapidly when planted in the spring, so late June and early July seedlings for fall production are most suitable.

Michihli forms a tall slender head. Wong-bok, Hybrid G, and Burpee Hybrid have shorter, blockier heads. Crispy Choy is a non-heading or looseleaf type.

Green and purple types of kohlrabi dug after partially overwintering in a garden in Oregon.

The Popular, Cultivated Tomato And Kinfolk Peppers, Eggplant

by Allan K. Stoner and Benigno Villalon

Tomatoes, peppers and eggplant are all members of the same family. Since they require virtually the same climatic and cultural conditions to grow in the home garden, they will be discussed together. These are considered warm season crops. Thus they are suited to spring, summer, and autumn culture over most of the North and upper South and they will grow in the winter in the extreme South.

Tomatoes are probably the most popular garden vegetable grown in the United States. This can be attributed to their unique flavor, attractiveness, richness as a source of vitamins C and A, and versatility as a food. The popularity of peppers can be attributed to the same factors, although they are usually not consumed in large enough quantities to make them an important nutritional factor in the diet.

The cultivated tomato, *Lycopersicon esculentum* Mill., originated in the Andes mountains of South America. It was introduced to other areas of the world by Indians and European travelers. The first report of the tomato in North America was in 1710 where it was grown primarily as an ornamental plant. Tomatoes began gaining wide acceptance as a food plant in the United States between 1820 and 1850.

Peppers are also native to tropical America and were grown by American Indian tribes in both North and South America over 2,000 years ago. The small red hot peppers were discovered by Columbus in the West

Allan K. Stoner is Research Horticulturist, U.S. Department of Agriculture, Beltsville, Md., and Benigno Villalon is Assistant Professor, Texas Agricultural Experiment Station, Weslaco.

Indies and introduced into Europe where they became popular before gaining widespread acceptance in the United States. Peppers became one of the first New World foods used commercially in Europe.

Pepper varieties grown in the United States are grouped in *Capsicum annum*, with the only exception being the red hot tabasco pepper *Capsicum frutescens* imported from the state of Tabasco, Mexico.

Eggplant, *Solanum melongena*, is believed to be native to India. It apparently moved into the Mediterranean area during the Dark Ages and was later introduced into America by the Spaniards.

Probably the most important step for the gardener in growing tomatoes or peppers is to select the proper varieties to plant. Many varieties of both crops are well adapted for home gardens.

A good garden tomato variety should possess resistance to as many of the commonly occurring diseases as possible, and resistance to growth cracks and bursting caused by alternating dry and wet weather. It should also be adapted to the local environmental and soil conditions and produce attractive fruit with good flavor and high nutritional value.

Resistance to verticillium wilt, fusarium wilt and nematodes is often indicated by including a V, F, N with the name. Nematode resistance is normally only required in Southern and some Western areas while V and F resistance is likely to be important in most areas.

Generally, gardeners should grow varieties with an indeterminate type of vine that will continue to grow and set fruit over a long period of time. Determinate varieties that set and

139

ripen all their fruits at nearly the same time are ideal for home canning when you want a lot of tomatoes at one time.

In addition to different vine types, the gardener can choose from small "cherry" to large "beefsteak" varieties. Varieties range in ripe fruit color from yellow to orange, pink, and bright red, and vary in fruit shapes.

New tomato varieties are released by seed companies and State and Federal experiment stations each year. You can obtain information about adapted varieties from seed catalogs, local nurserymen, county agricultural agents, newspaper and magazine garden articles, and successful neighborhood gardeners.

Pepper Groupings

Pepper varieties are easily classified as sweet, mild or hot depending on the amount of the heat or pungent compound, capsaicin, present in the fruit. However, there are many different common or commercial names for the hundreds of fruit types and shapes.

The horticultural varietal grouping that follows helps in understanding pepper fruit diversity even though varieties within the groups may be completely unrelated.

Bell Group fruits are large, blocky, about 3 inches wide by 4 inches long, 3- to 4-lobed, and taper slightly. Most are dark green, turning bright red at maturity, although some turn yellow. The California Wonder sweet types are probably the most popular garden peppers in the United States. There are also some hot bells. There may be upwards of 200 open pollinated and hybrid varieties in this group.

Cayenne Group—This is the chili group characterized by slim, pointed, hot or mild, slightly curved fruit pods, 2 to 12 inches long. The largest fruited varieties in this group are the Anaheim or New Mexico chili whose pods are 6 to 12 inches long. These are

used in the green stage for chili relleno or mild green sauce. The fully matured red dry pod is used in making red chopped chili pepper, ground chili powder, paprika if the variety is sweet, and oleoresin.

The Cayenne is 4 to 12 inches long, pointed, wrinkled, deep red, dry at maturity and used primarily in making hot sauce. The small hot peppers include the 2-inch pointed, slim red chili used in hot sauces, and the bullet-shaped 1½-inch to 2½-inch chubby Serrano eaten green in fresh salads or sauces. Probably the most popular of all the small hot peppers is the pungent jalapeno. It is conical, 2 to 3 inches long with a blunt point, an inch to 1½ inches wide at the shoulders, with thick walls. Jalapenos may be eaten fresh but most are canned by a process called "escabeche".

Perfection or Pimiento Group fruits are sweet, conical, slightly pointed, 2 to 3 inches wide and 3 to 4 inches long, with thick red walls. Popular pimiento varieties include Bighart, Truhart Perfection, and Pimiento L. These are primarily used for canning, stuffing olives, cheeses, etc., but can be used fresh in salads for flavor and color.

Celestial Group fruits are produced upright or erect, cone shaped, ¾ inch to 2 inches long, 3-celled, and colors may or may not change from yellowish to red or purplish to light orange-red. Different colors may appear on the same plant simultaneously, making them an attractive ornamental plant. Popular varieties include Floral Gem, Fresno chili, and Celestial.

Tabasco Group fruits are an inch to 3 inches long, slim, tapered, and very hot. Tabasco is the most popular variety in this group. Others include Japanese Cluster, Coral Gem, Chili Piquin, Small Red Chili, and very small Cayenne. They are used in sauces, for pickling, and are attractive ornamentals.

Cherry Group fruits are cherry-shaped or globose, 3-celled, borne on long slender, upright pedicels more or less above the leaves. Fruit may be orange to deep red, sweet or hot, large or small. They are attractive as ornamentals and are used for pungent seasoning. Popular varieties include Bird's Eye, Red Cherry Small, and Red Cherry Large.

Tomato Group fruits are distinctly flattened or oblate, 4-celled, and bear a striking resemblance to a tomato. These are used for pickling, canning, or fresh pepper rings. Varieties include Sunnybrook, Topepo, and Tomato.

Compared to tomatoes and peppers, there are relatively few eggplant varieties. Large fruited varieties are most commonly grown in the United States; however, many gardeners and cooks consider them inferior in quality to the small-fruited varieties. Gardeners in Northern areas with a short growing season must be especially aware of the number of days required for a variety to reach maturity. Eggplant varieties also differ in the shape and color of their fruits.

Planting, Fertilizing

Plant tomatoes, peppers and eggplants where they will receive a maximum amount of direct sunlight. A fertile, well-drained soil is required for best results. If the soil is not naturally fertile, fertilize it, preferably with a combination of manure and commercial fertilizer. All three crops are moderately tolerant to an acid soil (pH 5.5 to 6.8), but strongly acid soils should be limed according to soil test recommendations.

Fertilize tomatoes, peppers and eggplants in about the same way. However, since it is more important that peppers and eggplants start quickly and grow rapidly after transplanting, give them a little more nitrogen and potassium. If peppers or eggplants start blooming and set fruit

Teaspoon of all-purpose fertilizer (5-10-5 or 10-6-4) applied to planting hole at planting time will give your tomato plants a good start.

while the plants are too small, they will be stunted and fail to develop the plant size needed for a good yield.

On loam and heavier soils of fair to good fertility, 5 to 8 pounds of 5-10-5 fertilizer per 500 square feet should be mixed with the soil about a week before transplanting. On lighter or more sandy soils, 10 to 20 pounds of 5-10-5 per 500 square feet should be incorporated into the soil before planting. When the plants have set several fruits, apply a topdressing of the same type of fertilizer to prevent the plants from slowing down in vegetative growth. If the soil is very low in fertility, you may need to fertilize more frequently. Poor foliage color and stunted growth call for additional fertilizer.

Tomatoes, peppers, and eggplants need water in an amount equal to that provided by a 1-inch rain each week during the growing season. If rainfall is deficient or you live in an arid area, soak the plants thoroughly once a week. If the soil is sandy, you may need to water more frequently. Heavy soakings at weekly intervals are better than many light sprinklings. Tomatoes, peppers and eggplant respond very well to trickle or drip irrigation also.

Peppers particularly need abundant water during flowering and fruit set to prevent shedding of flowers and small fruits.

Transplanting

Tomatoes, peppers, and eggplant may be seeded directly into the garden in areas with a long growing season, but transplanting into the garden generally is recommended. Prior to direct seeding, work the soil into a somewhat granular condition. After planting, keep the soil moist until the seeds germinate. If the seeds are sown thick to insure getting a good plant stand, thin the seedlings to the proper spacing by the time they have three leaves. When early tomatoes, peppers or eggplants are desired, or the growing season is likely to be too short for heavy yields, use purchased or home grown transplants. A chapter about transplants begins on Page 111.

Tomatoes can be safely planted outside on the frost-free date, but because peppers and eggplant are somewhat more exacting in their temperature requirements than tomatoes, they should not be planted in the garden until a week or more after the frost-free date. A good general rule is to transplant outside when the new leaves on oak trees are fully grown.

Stake tomato plants before they get too large and before roots can be damaged by stake.

William E. Carnahan

Norman A. Plate

If there is danger of frost after the plants are put outside, protect them with paper or plastic coverings, newspapers, or boxes. Remove the covers during the day.

Set tomato plants into the garden at about the same depth as they were growing indoors. You don't need to remove the growing containers if they are made of peat or paper. If clay containers were used, knock the plants out of the pots before transplanting.

After transplanting, press the soil firmly around the plant so that a slight depression is formed to hold water. Then pour about a pint of water (to which fertilizer has been added) around each plant. Use 2 tablespoons of granular 5-10-5 fertilizer per gallon of water or a water-soluble starter fertilizer.

Plant peppers and eggplants in rows 30 to 42 inches apart and spaced 12 to 18 inches apart in the row.

Distances between tomato plants depend on the variety used and whether they are to be pruned and staked. Staked plants should be 18 inches apart in rows 3 feet apart. Unstaked plants should be 3 feet apart in rows 4 to 5 feet apart.

Staking or supporting tomatoes makes it easier to cultivate and harvest, and helps prevent fruit rots by keeping the fruits from coming in contact with soil. However, staked

Tomato plants in wire cages. Be sure openings are large enough so you can pick fruit. Cages are stored in off-season for re-use.

143

plants are more subject to losses from blossom-end rot than unstaked plants. Due to the woody nature of pepper and eggplant stems, you don't have to stake or support these crops.

If you plan to stake your tomatoes, insert the stakes soon after transplanting to prevent root damage. Wood stakes about 6 to 8 feet long and 1½ inches wide can be used. Push the stakes into the soil about 2 feet.

Tie soft twine or strips of rag tightly around the stake 2 to 3 inches above a leaf stem, then loop the twine loosely around the main stem not far below the base of the leaf stem, and tie with a square knot. Plant ties, made of tape reinforced with wire, may also be used to fasten plants to stakes. Six-inch mesh concrete reinforcing wire may also be used to support tomato plants by forming a circle 18 inches in diameter around the plant.

If you wish to prune staked tomato plants to 1 or 2 stems, about once a week remove by hand the small shoots that appear at the point where the leaf stem joins the main stem. Grasp the shoot with your thumb and forefinger and bend it sharply to one side until it snaps, then pull it off in the opposite direction.

Weed Control

The area around tomatoes, peppers, and eggplants should be kept free of weeds because of competition for sunlight, soil nutrients, and water. You can do this by mulching, hand pulling, or cultivating not more than 1 to 2 inches deep. Pepper and eggplant roots are particularly slow growing; thus any amount of root pruning can cause stunted growth and flowers to drop. Avoid cultivation when the soil is wet since it can lead to clumping of the soil and soil compaction.

Several insect species damage tomatoes including flea beetles,

tomato fruitworms, hornworms, aphids, leafminers, pinworms, Colorado potato beetles, whitefly, and spider mites. In small gardens some of these can be controlled by hand picking them from the plants. The others can be controlled by using approved insecticides at the proper time.

Two of the most common tomato diseases occurring in home gardens are fusarium and verticillium wilts. They are caused by fungi that live in the soil. Before the development of resistant varieties, gardeners were urged to plant in a different part of the garden each year; this is still a good idea. The best control, however, is to grow resistant varieties. Spraying or dusting is ineffective in controlling either of the wilt diseases.

Blossom-end rot is the most troublesome fruit rot for the home gardener. It is caused by a calcium deficiency and is aggravated by any kind of drought stress on the plants. Calcium, in the form of finely ground dolomitric limestone, will help prevent blossom-end rot. It must be applied before tomatoes are planted.

Other fruit rots are caused by fungi. Usually these fruit rots are not a problem when plants are staked. Most fruit rots can be controlled either by spraying with a fungicide or mulching with a suitable material such as black plastic. In areas where the leaves are frequently wet because of rain or dew, leaf spot diseases such

Tomato hornworm damages foliage and fruit on tomatoes, eggplants, and peppers.

as early blight, late blight, gray leaf spot or septoria leaf spot can be destructive. These can be controlled by applying a suitable fungicide at 7- to 10-day intervals. Wetting the foliage when watering can accentuate these diseases.

Virus diseases can cause a mottled discoloration of tomato foliage and occasionally a mottling of the fruit. Since tobacco mosaic virus is transmitted by direct contact, wash your hands and tools before touching the plants. Do not smoke while handling tomato, pepper, and eggplant plants.

Cucumber mosaic virus is transmitted by aphids that may be harbored in some perennial flowers or in nearby weeds. Cucumber mosaic can be controlled by eradicating perennial weeds and by spraying the tomato plants with an insecticide that controls aphids.

Tomatoes are subject to damage by many species of nematodes, but root-knot nematodes are the most troublesome. Affected plants become yellow and stunted and their roots can be galled, pruned, matted, or decayed. If nematodes are known to be present in damaging numbers based on the experience of previous years, they should be controlled before tomatoes are planted. Nematode control can be obtained by using an approved nematicide.

Insects attacking peppers—such as leaf miners, aphids, budworms, flea beetles, hornworms, pepper weevils, cutworms, and the pepper maggot— can be controlled with timely applications of insecticides used according to the manufacturer's directions.

Common pepper diseases include seedling damping off, bacterial leaf spot, Cercospora leaf spot, Phytophthora root rot, and mosaic virus diseases. Seed treatment and applications of fungicides or soil fumigation can help reduce losses. Several fungicides give adequate control of most leaf spot diseases.

Mosaic virus diseases such as tobacco etch virus, potato virus Y, tobacco mosaic, cucumber mosaic and tobacco ringspot virus can only be controlled by using resistant varieties. There are many pepper varieties resistant to tobacco mosaic, but very few resistant to tobacco etch and potato virus Y, and none to cucumber mosaic or tobacco ringspot virus. The release of multiple virus resistant pepper varieties can be anticipated in the future.

Phomopsis rot and verticillium wilt are two serious diseases of eggplants. The Phomopsis rot is characterized by large sunken, tan-colored or black areas on the fruits. It may also cause canker-like lesions on the lower part of the stem and leaf spots which may enlarge until the whole leaf turns brown. The disease may be carried over winter by debris in the soil from the previous crop. To control fruit rot, use clean seed, practice a 3- to 4-year crop rotation, and grow rot-resistant varieties.

Verticillium wilt of eggplant is particularly common in cooler regions and is similar in its behavior to wilt disease of tomato. It seems to persist in the soil indefinitely, and can be distributed by plants from infested seedbeds. Wilt injury ranges from stunting, with decreased productivity, to death of the plant.

Several insects attack eggplants, particularly flea beetles, aphids, lace bugs, and sometimes the Colorado potato beetle. Red spiders occasionally become troublesome on eggplants, especially during dry weather.

Harvesting

To obtain the best flavor and color, harvest tomatoes after they are fully ripe. Tomatoes can be expected to ripen 60 to 90 days after transpalnting. If picked green, they can be ripened at temperatures between 55° and 72° F. Light will increase the color of tomatoes somewhat, but light

Eggplant nearly ready for harvesting.

is not essential to ripening. When tomatoes are placed in direct sunlight to ripen, the added heat often lowers their quality.

Green sweet peppers are harvested when they reach a good usable size and still retain their dark green color. Immature peppers are soft and yield readily to mild pressure of the fingers. Red peppers, either sweet or hot, are allowed to develop full red color before picking. Hot peppers can be harvested early for green sauce or canning or allowed to ripen, then harvested.

Pepper fruit will be ready for harvesting between 70 days for early green fruits to 130 days for some of the fully mature red pods. Peppers are generally harvested by breaking them from the plant with the stems left attached to the fruits.

Eggplants may be harvested any time after they have reached sufficient size, but before the skin color becomes dull, the flesh tough, and the seeds begin to harden. Most varieties will be ready for the first harvest in 85 to 90 days after transplanting.

Harvest eggplants by cutting the tough stems with a sharp knife.

Per plant yields for the various crops will vary greatly depending on the variety, the growing season, the area of the country, and the cultural practices you follow. However, it is reasonable to expect tomatoes to yield 10 to 14 pounds per plant, peppers to yield 1 pound per plant, and you can anticipate 4 to 8 eggplants per plant.

Leafy Salad Vegetables: Lettuce, Celery, Cress, Endive, Escarole, Chicory

by Bruce Johnstone

The principal leafy salad vegetables covered in this chapter, especially lettuce, are among the most widely grown vegetables by home gardeners throughout the United States. Most of them—but not celery and chicory—are easy and fast to grow, and with the exception of celery are among the relatively few vegetables that tolerate moderate shade.

They also are adapted to small home gardens because each of them requires but little space for an average size crop. Salad crops in general also conform to the currently popular American taste for low calorie and high vitamin content foods.

Besides the leafy salad crops covered in this chapter—lettuce, celery, cress, endive, escarole and chicory—a few other leafy vegetables covered under different categories and in separate chapters also can be used advantageously as green leafy ingredients in salad making. Among these are spinach, New Zealand spinach, chard and mustard, each adding a slightly different flavor, color and texture to various salads.

Other common salad vegetables such as tomatoes, cucumbers, onions and radishes are covered in different chapters of this book and can be located through the table of contents or the index.

Lettuce

Known botanically as *Lactuca sativa* of the Composite family, lettuce probably originated somewhere in Asia Minor and the eastern Mediterranean region. Used as a food plant for some 2,500 years, it was a favorite of Persian kings in the sixth century B.C. and later as a food plant by the Romans. In the late 15th century, it first was brought to the New World by Columbus.

Lettuce seed is rather small (25,000 seeds per ounce), germinates quickly (7 days) in cool (65°-70° F) temperature, and produces a crop comparatively fast. Loose leaf lettuce types normally produce a crop in 40 to 50 days while most heading varieties require 60 to 80 days to mature.

The loose leaf varieties are more widely grown than heading types in home gardens because they are faster to mature, easier to grow, and somewhat more shade tolerant. They also have about three times as much vitamin A and roughly six times as much ascorbic acid or vitamin C as the equivalent amount of the heading varieties. Loose leaf varieties of lettuce require less thinning and thrive under somewhat warmer and more adverse conditions than the heading types.

Because lettuce basically is a cool weather crop, seed should be sown direct in the garden in early spring in order to mature before the summer heat arrives to cause bolting and deterioration of the foliage. (Bolting is premature flowering). Five feet of row per adult in family is usually enough for each planting.

Successive plantings can be made in midsummer for autumn crops.

The seed should be scattered thinly, covered a quarter inch deep in rows as close as 8 and up to 24 inches apart, depending on space available.

Thinning is not absolutely necessary for loose leaf kinds but spacing the plants 4 to 6 inches apart is com-

Bruce Johnstone of Excelsior, Minn., retired as chief horticulturist at Northrup, King & Co. He co-authored *Vegetable Gardening From the Ground Up*, a paperback book, in 1976, and *America's Most Beautiful Flowers* in 1977.

S. Goto

monly recommended and results in larger, more easily harvested leaves. Typical loose leaf varieties available are: Black Seeded Simpson, Grand Rapids and Salad Bowl.

Heading varieties are of two main types, crisphead and butterhead. Crisphead varieties are of thinner texture, are crisp, frequently have curled and serrated edges, are harder and more durable in handling and storage. Most of the so called Iceberg types available in stores are of this class. Other typical crisphead varieties: Ithaca, Great Lakes 118 and 659.

In contrast, butterhead types are softer and more fragile in texture, have thicker leaves and a smooth, buttery substance. Butterhead types— Bibb, Buttercrunch, White Boston— have a distinct delicate flavor and usually are more perishable than the crisphead varieties.

Heading varieties have cultural requirements similar to the loosehead types of lettuce except they require a longer, cooler growing season, more careful thinning, and need full sun for best development. All lettuce types are heavy feeders and because of their limited root structure require ample and constant soil moisture. They need high nitrogen fertility in a moist soil and give best results if growth continues unchecked.

Cos lettuce (Romaine) or celery lettuce has an elongated framework, smooth outer leaves, and a blanched inner head. The leaves are more brittle than the other heading types, the midrib is heavier, and the flavor uniquely sweet and mild. Cos types usually take 65 to 70 days to mature and have the same basic planting and cultural requirements as the other heading types. Most popular varieties are Paris White Cos and Paris Island Cos.

Where there are short, hot growing seasons as in much of our Northern, Central and Midwest states, the heading varieties are most successfully grown by starting seed indoors in very early spring, then getting the transplants into the garden as soon as frost danger is past. In this way the plants can mature and form heads

Left, young gardener checks lettuce in her garden in Hawaii. Right, Bibb lettuce being harvested.

before summer heat curtails growth and development.

Harvest with a sharp knife as soon as looseleaf types are the size of your hand. Heading varieties should be full and firm. If allowed to go to seed in warm weather, leaves lose quality and become bitter.

When cultivating or hoeing lettuce, take care to keep the blade shallow and not too close to the plants to avoid injuring the root system which is sparse and close to the surface.

Homegrown lettuce is relatively free of disease although leafhoppers can be a problem, mostly in spreading virus disease. Effective chemical controls are available.

Celery

Celery (Apium graveolens—family Umbelliferae) is native to marshy areas from Scandinavia to Algeria and Egypt and eastward to the Caucasus and into Baluchistan and parts of India.

The two main classes of celery are the green and the golden, or self-blanching. The green type with unblanched stalks adds considerably to the appearance and flavor of both salads and casseroles and is currently more popular on American tables. This type includes Giant Pascal, Forkhook and Utah strains. For use as a canape of raw vegetables, some cooks still prefer the golden or self-blanching type with yellowish white stalks and usually a milder, blander favor. Popular golden varieties grown are Golden Plume, Cornell 19 and Michigan Golden.

Celery seed is very small (60,000 per ounce) compared with other common vegetables, very slow to germinate (15 to 21 days) and requires a long, cool growing season of 120 to 140 days to produce a crop.

Celery needs a rich, moist soil and mild, equable growing conditions without sudden cold spells or dry periods to check its growth. Muck or sandy loam soils with good fertility are ideal. These exacting conditions make celery growing by home gardeners rather difficult, especially in much of the Midwest and inland Northern areas. In coastal regions or areas near large bodies of water, the usually longer and more temperate growing conditions are more suitable for celery culture.

Because celery is such a slow growing, rather difficult crop to raise, it should not ordinarily be chosen by a beginning gardener in most areas. It is successfully produced, however, by many experienced gardeners in favorable areas who take the time and care necessary. Because of its many culinary uses from salads to casseroles to attractive canapes, it probably is well worth the effort.

Celery seed must be started very early (usually indoors) 8 to 10 weeks before spring planting time unless commercially grown transplants are available. Germination is very slow, usually 2 to 3 weeks, and can be hastened slightly by presoaking the seed

Celery display in a garden.

overnight before sowing in flats 1/16 inch deep. Seed flats must be kept moist and covered at 60° to 70° F temperature until the sprouts appear.

At this stage, they should be uncovered immediately and moved to direct sunlight and a slightly cooler situation. Seedlings must be transplanted or thinned so that developing plants are 1½ to 2 inches apart and kept in full sunlight until frost-free planting time. The young plants then can be hardened off outdoors, and set in the garden, spacing them 6 to 10 inches apart in rows 2 feet apart.

For ordinary usage, figure on a half-dozen plants per adult in family. Harvest by cutting at base of stalk with a sharp knife. The usual harvest span is from the stage when the stalk is two-thirds of full size until fully would be about a 5-10-10 ratio.

Celery requires ample and continuous soil moisture and a high fertility. If soil is not rich, fertilizer should be used. The formula depends on the individual soil type, but in most cases would be about a 5-10-10 ratio.

Celery may be attacked by leaf-eating worms and aphids (plant lice). You can control these insects with approved insecticides. Blight and mildew also may be problems; control them with an appropriate fungicide.

Endive—Escarole

Endive (Cichorium endivia—family Compositae) is native to regions of the eastern Mediterranean and was grown and used by Greeks and Egyptians before the Christian era. Closely related to chicory, endive has small seeds (27,000 per ounce) which germinate quickly (5 to 14 days) under moist conditions and in varying temperatures from 60° to 70° F.

There are two principal types of endive: Curled or Curly—with loose, narrow, medium green fringed and curly leaves; and Batavian or escarole with broader, thicker, smooth leaves that have a white midrib forming a loose head with partly blanched inner foliage.

Endive is more tolerant of summer heat and low soil moisture than most lettuce varieties, and is also slower to grow and mature (usually 85 to 95 days). The curled varieties can be cut and cropped, yet continue to produce new secondary edible leaves. These curled varieties such as Green Curled, Ruffec, and Deep Heart have a slightly bitter flavor but are very decorative and desirable in salads and for garnish. The broad-leaved Batavian or escarole varieties are somewhat milder and add a different flavor and texture to salads.

Seed is usually sown direct in the garden in the early spring ¼ inch deep in rows 2 to 3 feet apart, later thinned to 6 or 8 inches between plants. Four to five feet of row per adult in family will suffice for average table use.

For earlier harvest, seed may be started in flats indoors 6 to 8 weeks before planting time, then transplanted to the garden. Summer sowing of seed will produce autumn crops which, maturing in cooler weather, are apt to be somewhat milder in flavor and with less of the slight bitterness characteristic of summer harvested crops. Loosely tying the outer leaves upright to exclude sunlight tends to blanch the inner leaves, making them milder and reducing the bitter taste.

Harvest by cutting at base or carefully pulling entire plant when inner leaves are partly or wholly blanched. Outer leaves are apt to be bitter and usually are discarded.

Endive seldom is bothered by insects or disease problems. Sometimes, in mild damp areas, slugs or snails may appear and eat the foliage. Control them with special snail bait or slug protectant. Dry ashes around plants usually repel both slugs and snails.

Cress

Garden Cress or pepper grass (*Lepidium sativum*) belongs to the Cruciferae family and although similar in flavor to water cress and upland cress, it is far more popular and much easier to grow under ordinary gardening conditions. Water Cress (*Nasturtium officinale*) is a semi-aquatic plant requiring very cold spring water conditions to grow well. Upland Cress (*Barbarea verna*) tolerates a normal soil but is slower to grow, somewhat bitter in taste, and not commonly produced in U. S. gardens.

Garden Cress is both easy to grow and extremely fast to form edible leaves. The seeds are moderate in size (12,000 per ounce) and under moderate temperature of 65° to 70° germinate in 4 to 7 days.

Garden cress is probably the fastest seed to sprout of all garden vegetables. The young seedlings also grow rapidly and the very young immature leaves are tender, mildly pungent like water cress, and they can be cropped for table use when only a few inches high—10 days to 2 weeks old.

Garden cress is used commonly as a quick growing indoor crop, often available in preseeded kits with a medium of vermiculite, peat moss, etc., and is intended to be grown in a sunny kitchen window to produce edible leaves in 10 to 15 days. Grown this way indoors, cress can be available and used all winter long by successive plantings.

Outdoor spring and summer garden culture is also easy enough but for continued harvest one must make successive plantings every few weeks. Hot summer weather causes garden cress plants to bolt quickly and lose quality, so early cropping is necessary.

Sow the seed ¼ inch deep in rows a foot apart and harvest as soon as seedlings are 3 to 4 inches high for the best quality.

A 10- to 15-foot row usually suffices for the average family. Cut with a sharp knife as soon as leaves are formed.

Chicory

Chicory (*Cichorium intybus*—family Compositae), also known as French Endive or Witloof Chicory, is thought to be native to Europe and Asia. Although some chicory is grown for the roots which are dried, ground and used as a coffee adulerant, we will cover here the salad type and culture in which the blanched leaves are the garden crop wanted.

Chicory is related closely to endive but usually produced in a far different manner.

The seeds are small (27,000 per ounce) and they germinate in 7 to 14 days at temperatures between 68° to 85° R.

Seed ordinarily is spring sown a quarter inch deep in 15- to 18-inch rows and the seedlings thinned to eventually stand 4 to 5 inches apart. It must not be planted too early or premature flowering (bolting) will occur.

The parsnip-like roots are harvested in the fall before freezing weather, washed, and trimmed of all leaves except the single central crown bud on top. The roots are then stored under cover in a cool frost-free room.

These roots are stored and later planted for winter production of the edible shoots by setting them slantwise at a depth of 4 to 6 inches with crowns about even with the surface in a medium of sand, sawdust or a similar porous medium at temperatures of 50° to 60° F in a dark place. In 3 to 4 weeks the blanched heads or shoots appear and are ready to cut and harvest. Successive winter plantings of the stored dormant roots every 2 to 3 weeks can be made to produce edible shoots throughout the winter.

Onions Are Finicky as to Growing, Curing; And Garlic May Not Be a Joy Either

by J. S. Vandemark

Onions are grown in nearly every part of the United States. Fairly cool temperatures are important during early development, and good soil fertility and adequate moisture are essential. High temperatures help during bulbing and curing. Low humidity is desirable for curing.

Domesticated in Asia and the Middle East, onions were rapidly moved to Europe. They were grown both by the settlers and Indians after being brought to North America by Spanish explorers.

Onions are used in a variety of forms. They are eaten raw, as scallions, and in salads. Cooked onions are served broiled, boiled, baked, creamed, steamed, fried, french fried, pickled, in soups and stews, and in combinations with other vegetables and meats.

Growers learned from experience that the early development period of onions should be cool and damp to allow secondary roots to develop.

Soil fertilization should be given particular attention. Onions require about twice as much fertilizer as most vegetables. Gardeners may find it advantageous to give the row a second feeding after 40 to 60 days by placing the fertilizer in a trench 1 to 2 inches deep and 3 inches to one side of the row. Use 10-10-10 fertilizer at a rate of 1 pound per 25 or 30 feet of row for this sidedressing.

Good growth requires a loose, friable (crumbly), fertile soil. Hard compact soils tend to restrain bulb development, causing the bulb to be irregularly shaped and small.

Proper time to plant depends on the area. In the South, onions are grown in winter, from seeds, sets or seedlings that were fall-planted. In Northern and Central regions, onions are planted in spring as early as the soil can be prepared. Onions are tolerant to frosts. Seeds germinate best about 60° to 65° F; however, satisfactory results will be obtained anywhere from 50° to 75° soil temperature.

Onions must be kept free of weeds and grasses throughout the entire season as they compete poorly with other plants.

Onions From Sets

Onion sets are the surest route to success in the home vegetable garden as the emerging plant will be vigorous and strong. They may serve double duty, producing green onions or mature dry onions. Onion sets, which you can buy, consist of small dry onions up to ¾ inch in diameter grown the previous year specifically for starting plants.

Select sets early when they are firm and dormant. While it seems contradictory, round onion sets produce flat onions, while elongated or tapered sets mature into round onions. Sets are available in three colors: White, red or brown. Most gardeners prefer white sets for producing green onions or scallions; but the other two colors are acceptable.

Divide the sets into two groups, those smaller in diameter than a dime and those larger 'than a dime. Use large size sets for green onions; the large size may bolt (form flower stalks) and not produce a good dry bulb.

Plant the small size set for dry onion production as there is little chance of bolting. These small sets will best produce large, dry bulbs.

J. S. Vandemark is Vegetable Crop Specialist, University of Illinois, Urbana.

For dry onions, plant the sets to a depth of 1 inch in rows 12 to 14 inches apart, with the sets 2 inches apart. Soil should be worked to a medium fine condition, fertilized, and kept free of weeds throughout the season.

When you observe half or more of the tops bent over naturally, the onions may be pulled and allowed to dry. Do not break onion stems early as this interrupts their natural growth period and will result in reducing the bulb size. Onions can be eaten at any point between green onions and mature dry onions.

When planting larger size bulbs for green onions, use 12- to 24-inch wide rows. Sets can be planted close enough to touch each other and 1½ inches deep. If you hill the row slightly after the stem is up 4 inches, the green onions will have longer usable white stems. Once the tops are 6 inches high you can start using them as green onions.

Green onions become stronger in flavor as they get older. When too strong to eat raw, they are excellent for cooking.

If you notice a plant producing a flower stalk (bolting), pull and use it.

Seed is the least popular method of growing, as a longer period for development is needed. Onion seed should be planted at the same time as sets and requires similar fertilization. To assure a good stand, plant seed ¾ to 1 inch deep, at a rate of 1 to 5 seeds per inch. When the seedlings are established they should be thinned: For large dry onions 2 to 3 inches apart, for medium sized 1 to 2 inches, and for boilers and green onions, ¼ to 1 inch.

Choose varieties adapted to your purpose and section of the country. Green onion varieties from seed include Evergreen Bunching, Beltsville Bunching, and Southport Bunching. Varieties for dry onions produced in the South include Crystal Wax, Excel,

Texas Grano, and Granex. In the North suitable varieties are Early Yellow Globe, Empire, Fiesta, Downing Yellow Globe, Spartan lines, and Nutmeg.

Onions From Transplants

Transplanting of young onion plants is an increasingly popular method for home gardeners because of the large size bulb produced. Plants may be obtained from your seed dealer and garden supplier. In the South and Southwest plant in fall, and in the North in early spring. To produce large dry onions, plant 4 to 5 inches apart in the row, with rows 12 to 24 inches apart. Closer spacing yields smaller size bulbs. Fertile, loose soil is essential.

Transplants are put in soil to a depth of 1 to 1½ inches and covered. Many growers use a special water-soluble fertilizer mixture immediately on planting.

This transplant fertilizer is in addition to the normal fertilizing of the garden and the necessary sidedressing discussed earlier. To prepare a water fertilizer mixture, buy a soluble fertilizer, 10-50-10, 10-52-17, or similar analysis. Dissolve one tablespoon in a gallon of water and apply at the rate of 1 cup per plant.

Crystal Wax, Bermudas, and Grano types are used in the South for fall planting. In the North, Bermudas are used when flat bulbs are desired. For large round bulbs use standard or hybrid Sweet Spanish (white or yellow). If red onions are preferred, varieties like Red Bermudas, Red Giant, Red Hamburger, and Benny's Red are used in the North, while Early Red or Creole are suitable for the South.

Special onions include the *Egyptian onion* or tree onion, a perennial planted in fall throughout the country. This onion forms small bulblets or sets where the flowers normally grow. It may be harvested, planted and used in the same manner as sets.

David Warren

Hanging onions for curing.

In late winter or early spring, Egyptian onions may be pulled and used as green onions. Those left unharvested will produce new sets for future planting. If you choose, the plants also may be dug, divided, and replanted for additional propagation. Planting material, either sets or plants, are hard to get through normal channels and often gardeners obtain their starts from friends.

The *Potato or Multiplier onion* seldom produces seed and is propagated by bulb division. These onions are planted in the same manner as sets, usually 2 to 3 inches apart. The original bulb splits into segments; when dry, they may be used to plant as sets.

In the South, multiplier sets are planted in fall and used as green onions in spring. In the North, they are planted early in spring.

True multipliers also are hard to get at most gardening centers, and like the Egyptian onion frequently are passed from gardener to gardener.

Many homeowners do not have proper conditions to store onions for long periods; however, they usually can make out all right for three to four months. After half of the tops have broken over naturally at the neck, the onions may be pulled. When the tops have wilted, cut them off 1 to 1½ inches above the bulb.

Cure by placing in an open crate or mesh bag. This process, which prepares the onions for storage, takes from two to a few weeks depending on humidity. Clean by removing dirt and outer loose dry skins that come off when handling.

The cleaned onion may be left in a mesh bag and hung in a place such as a garage ceiling. An ideal storage spot is dry with air temperatures of 35° to 50° F. If roots reappear, the conditions are too moist, and if sprouts appear the temperature is too high; either will cause rotting and deterioration of bulbs.

The storage period is shorter for Sweet Spanish and Bermudas than for small globe-type onions.

Offshoots of Onions

Garlic, shallots, chives and leeks are members of the onion family. These are often grown at home as they frequently are hard to obtain. Fertility and cultural practices are similar to those for onions.

Many areas will find *garlic* poorly adapted to home gardens.

Garlic produces a group of cloves that are encased in a sheath, rather than a single bulb. Separate into single cloves for planting.

The larger outer cloves produce the best garlic. These are planted 1 to 2 inches deep in a well fertilized garden, in rows 12 to 24 inches apart, with the cloves 5 to 6 inches apart. Planting is done in the South and Southwest from fall through January, and in the rest of the country as early in spring as possible. Delayed planting seriously reduces yield.

Harvest when the top dries down. To prepare garlic for storage, cure the bulbs under cool, dry conditions. Garlic may be stored under a wide range of temperatures, but does best under dry conditions with a temperature range of 40° to 60° F.

Shallots, prized by French chefs and gourmet cooks, are grown for either dry bulbs or young green shoots. They are harvested and used like green onions. Frequently writers confuse shallots with green onions, but shallots are a different species of the onion family.

The shallot bulb has multiple sections like garlic. These are separated and planted the same way you plant onion sets for dry bulbs, spaced 3 to 5 inches apart, with 12- to 24-inch rows.

In the South they are most often raised and used for the green portion, being planted in fall and harvested during winter. In the North, shallots are planted as early as possible in late winter or spring and used for both green onions and dry bulbs.

Seed shallots may be obtained from specialty seed stores or by purchasing dry shallot bulbs in the gourmet section of your food store and dividing into single segments for planting. Shallots are harvested, handled and stored like onions. Gardeners frequently save their own planting material from year to year.

Chives are a perennial member of the onion family and are grown for leaves, rather than bulb or stem. A small bulbous plant, chives grow in 6- to 10-inch clumps. Attractive violet flowers appear on older plants in spring.

Chives may be propagated by either dividing the clump or starting from seed. They are generally started from seed very early in spring.

After three years, large chive clumps should be subdivided in early spring to prevent overcrowding and a decline in vigor. The fertility program for chives is similar to that for onion transplants. Remove the flowers as they will cause the plant to be-

Top, clump of great headed (Elephant) garlic. Left, chives grown in kitchen window can be harvested as needed all year long.

Darrow M. Watt

come semi-dormant, preventing new growth.

Harvest chives any time there are fresh, young leaves. Young leaves may be chopped and frozen for future use. In late fall in the North many gardeners dig a clump of chives, allowing the exposed clump to freeze until mid-winter, and then bring the chives indoors for a fresh winter supply.

Leeks are grown as an annual, entirely from seed rather than plant divisions. The seed is planted in the garden or started in a hotbed for 2 to 3 months before transplanting to the garden. The young plants are set out in the South in fall and in the North in early spring. Leek transplants are handled in the same manner as onion transplants as regards fertility, transplant solution, and sidedressing.

The primary production difference from onions is that leeks are blanched by banking soil along the row gradually throughout the growing season. Exercise care when the plants are young as early banking may cause decay. Common varieties are American Flag, Conqueror, Tivi and Odin.

Leeks can be used any time the stems reach the size of ¾ to 1 inch in diameter. Before freezing in the North, they are harvested and stored in root cellars or placed in a polyethylene bag in the refrigerator. In parts of the country with open winters, they are allowed to remain in the garden and eaten as desired.

Left, leeks are used for almost any purpose that onions are. Right, leek seedlings being transplanted.

Root Crops More or Less Trouble-Free, Produce Lots of Food in a Small Space

by N. S. Mansour and J. R. Baggett

Root crops are valuable and satisfying additions to the garden because they offer a prolonged harvest season, long storage life, and produce a large amount of food in a small amount of space. With few exceptions, the root crops are trouble-free and do not require the continual care of other kinds of vegetables. They are also adapted to winter storage in root cellars or simple pits.

The table gives general characteristics of some of the root crops.

Root crops are best grown in well drained, loose friable (crumbly) soil. This is especially important because these crops are among the earliest planted and the latest harvested. If the soil is heavy, it may be beneficial to form a raised bed, 4 to 6 inches high and 12 to 24 inches across the top. The width of the top depends on whether 1 or 2 rows are planted on the bed. Use of raised beds reduces soil compaction during the growing season, permits easier digging, and allows carrots and parsnips to attain greater length and be smoother in shape.

Root crops, especially carrots and parsnips, tend to have fewer misshapen roots when grown on beds and will store better in the garden without splitting or rotting. Adding sand and humus to heavy soils will improve soil fertility and permit easier digging and cleaning of roots. However, adding sand without humus can cause a concrete-like condition.

Soil pH (acidity) is usually not limiting. But radishes, turnips, and rutabagas benefit from neutral or

---

N. S. Mansour is Extension Vegetable Crops Specialist, and J. R. Baggett is Professor of Horticulture, at Oregon State University, Corvallis.

slightly alkaline soils if club root disease is present. This disease is inhibited by an alkaline soil condition. You can reduce acidity by adding lime, at the rate of 15 to 20 pounds per hundred square feet of garden area.

A fertilizer rate of 2 pounds of 10-20-10 per hundred square feet of garden area is adequate; additional nitrogen may be required for celeriac. The fertilizer and lime should be thoroughly incorporated in the soil to a depth of 4 to 6 inches. Lime is best applied in fall. Don't use manure where carrots are to be grown, because misshapen roots can result.

Root crops may be planted as soon as the garden soil can be prepared. All have small seeds, which should be planted no deeper than ½ inch.

Crusting and drying can be minimized by mulching the seeded row with sawdust or bark dust, or using such materials as vermiculite or washed sand for covering the seeds instead of soil. Water the newly seeded rows frequently, as often as once a day, in order to prevent a crust from forming and to protect the tender seedlings from drying out until they are well established. Consult the table for appropriate thinning and spacing information.

Pests

Root crops do not often require pest control. However, radishes, turnips, and rutabagas can be seriously attacked by the cabbage maggot and control of this insect is important. The best prevention for the pest is treatment of the soil before planting with a suitable soil insecticide. This material can be spread over the garden area and gently raked into the top 1 or 2 inches of soil. Take care

Root Crop Characteristics

	Optimum monthly average growing temperature (Fahrenheit)		Optimum soil temperatures range for germination (Fahrenheit)	Frost tolerance	Spacing suggested in inches		Days to maturity	Time and frequency of planting	Harvest duration for each planting
	Min.	Max.			In row	Between rows			
Beets	40°	65°	50°–85°	Moderate	2–4	16–24	55–80	Early spring and early summer	2–3 months
Celeriac	45°	70°	60°–70°	Good	4–6	23–30	100–110 (56–84 for transplants)	Early spring only	3–6 weeks
Carrots	45°	70°	45°–85°	Moderate	1–3	16–24	60–85	Early spring and early summer	2–4 months
Parsnips	40°	75°	50°–70°	Good	3–6	18–30	100–130	Early spring only	3–4 months
Salsify	45°	85°	50°–90°	Good	2–4	18–30	150–155	Early spring only	1–2 months
Radishes (spring)	40°	75°	45°–90°	Good	½–1	9–18	25–30	Early spring and weekly	1 week
(winter)	40°	75°	45°–90°	Good	½–1	9–18	52–56	Early fall	3–5 weeks
Turnips	40°	75°	60°–95°	Good	2–6	12–30	45–75	Early spring and late summer	2–3 weeks
Rutabagas	40°	75°	50°–90°	Good	5–8	18–36	90–95	Early spring and midsummer	1–2 months

not to mix the insecticide too deeply into the soil since this will dilute it and reduce effectiveness.

You may need to drench turnips and rutabagas with an insecticide solution four to six weeks after planting, since the soil treatment can wear off by that time.

Control of aphids and flea beatles may sometimes be necessary.

Always consult the labels for application details of any pesticide.

Use of weed control chemicals is not feasible in most home gardens. Mulches are useful in reducing weeds after the crops have been well established. They are also useful in improving the color of carrots by preventing the green discoloration normally seen at shoulders of the root. Turnips and rutabagas should not be covered with a mulch if the typical purple color of the upper part of the root is desired.

There are usually no serious disease problems. The club root disease of radishes, turnips and rutabagas occurs only occasionally in gardens. Beets are sometimes seriously affected by canker, a non-parasitic disorder that occurs when there is boron deficiency in the soil.

Fungus and virus diseases of root crop foliage occasionally occur, but it is generally not necessary nor feasible for the gardener to attempt control.

Most root crops can be harvested over a wide range of maturity. Beets can be harvested when small or allowed to mature fully, and carrots can be used from pencil size to full grown over a period of three to six months. Spring radishes, a fast growing crop, are usable over a very short period. See table for days to maturity and harvest duration. Root crops often must be thinned if they are to mature properly and in the right length of time.

Mature root crops can be harvested and stored in a cool, moist location, but carrots, beets, parsnips and tur-

nips are best left in the garden area until severe frost is expected. They should then be pulled, topped, and stored in a cool, moist root cellar until needed for table use. Don't wash them until they are needed. In milder winter areas, leaving the roots in the ground is a practical storage method.

Root crops are relatively efficient as good producers for the space occupied. Twenty feet of row of each crop should produce an adequate quantity for a family of 4. Radishes, however, should be planted in short rows, preferably no more than 3 to 6 feet long, at weekly intervals. This will provide a steady supply of radishes throughout the season. Turnips also have a shorter life than most root crops and are best planted several times during the season.

The root crops are moderately high in vitamin C, with carrots an excellent source of vitamin A.

Radishes are a quick and easy crop to grow in a small space.

Notes on individual crops follow.

BEETS (*Beta vulgaris*)—Somewhat more susceptible to foliage diseases than the other root crops, and less tolerant of drought or low fertility than some, beets are still a relatively easy crop to grow.

Quality factors are not critical and although there may be a preference for small roots for whole pickles, beets are edible over a wide range of maturity. Young roots are more in-

tense in color, with less conspicuous light colored rings, more tender and finer textured.

Choice of varieties for gardens is not critical because a number of good ones of equal quality are available. However, if downy mildew is a problem, then look in seed catalogs for resistant varieties such as strains of popular Detroit Dark Red. Red beets are traditionally the most popular, but other types such as golden and white are also available. All have about the same potential flavor and quality.

CELERIAC (*Apium graveolens*, var. *rapaceum*)—A variant of common celery, celeriac produces heavy roots somewhat like a rutabaga in appearance. It is used raw in salads, pickled, or cooked in soups and stews. Good culture requires plenty of water and fertility and a long growing season. The use of transplants started indoors 10 weeks prior to outdoor planting time is superior over direct seeding.

Celeriac roots are used when they reach 2 to 3 inches in diameter, but have a long period of use and can be

Root crops in Oregon. Top right, Sakuri-jima Japanese radish left overwinter. Top left, three types of beets, Cylindra type, Crosby's Flat Egyptian type, and globe type, dug from garden in February. Bottom, American Purple Top rutabagas in garden in February.

160

stored with success. Few varieties are available.

CARROTS (*Daucus carota* L.)— Because of its nutritional value, bright orange color for the table, productivity, storage life and ease of culture, the carrot is a garden favorite.

If a problem is encountered with carrots, it is often failure to get a stand of seedlings. Carrots can not tolerate either deep planting or a dry seed bed, so the trick is to manage shallow planting with a continuously moist soil. Seeding at ¼-inch depth with a light mulch of sawdust and daily sprinkling is usually successful. If frequent, light irrigation is not possible, use a slightly deeper planting depth (to ½ inch).

Carrots are well adapted to culture in a wide row or bed instead of a single row. Seedlings should be thinned initially if there is not open space around each plant. Harvest of seedlings can begin when they are finger-size and continue through what will appear an inexhaustible supply, because the more the roots are pulled out, the larger the remaining ones will become.

Choose varieties to suit soil conditions. If the soil is deep and friable, any variety will do well and the very long market types such as Imperator or similar F_1 hybrids may be preferred. In heavy, impermeable soil, it is best to grow the shorter types such as the very adaptable Red Cored Chantenay, or even the stubby Oxheart. Nantes is a medium-long type which is tender and of good flavor, but susceptible to cracking and rotting in fall and generally not culturally rugged.

PARSNIPS (*Pastinaca sativa*)—Parsnips resemble carrots in cultural needs and the same suggestions for planting apply, except they should have more space for full development.

Parsnips are slower to mature, but have a long storage life, either in the ground or in the cellar. Drying out is

the greatest hazard in storage, so they should be surrounded by a moist medium or otherwise protected.

Roots left in the ground are remarkably resistant to decay and to freezing injury. Exposure to cold increases the sugar content and greatly enhances the flavor, but non-chilled roots are not poisonous as is sometimes supposed.

Because parsnip roots are very long, digging them in wet, heavy soil is a burden. Lightening the soil with sand and using raised beds makes digging and washing easier.

Only three varieties are normally available: Hollow Crown, Model and All America. All are satisfactory, though Model is smoother and less thinly tapered than Hollow Crown.

SALSIFY (*Tragopogon porrifolius*) —Used mostly for soup, in which it may have a faint oyster-like flavor, salsify or oyster plant is not frequently grown. Generally free from cultural problems, salsify has one disadvantage—the tendency for a branchy root which is difficult to clean and peel.

There is little or no choice of varieties in the United States. Mammoth Sandwich Island is usually listed.

Parsnip seedlings in early true stage.

161

SPRING RADISHES (*Raphanus sativus*)—This is the short-season, strictly annual type of radish. The term "spring radish" is somewhat misleading because these radishes can be grown throughout the season in cooler areas and in all but the hottest months in warmer climates.

Spring radishes live a very fast life, maturing and becoming pithy and unusable in a remarkably short time. Radish seeds germinate very rapidly and seedlings are fast and vigorous compared to those of most relatives in the cabbage family. They tolerate a wide range of conditions. However, hot, dry conditions encourage strong flavor and even faster maturing. Overcrowding results in small unusable roots. Overfertilization can cause excessive top growth at the expense of root enlargement. The most difficult problem for many gardeners is the cabbage root maggot. Control was discussed earlier in the chapter.

Many varieties of spring radishes are available, especially of the small red globe type. Comet, Sparkler, Cherry Belle, and Early Scarlet Globe are examples. Another distinct variety is the long White Icicle. There are also white globe types which are slightly larger and in some cases longer lasting than the red globe varieties. Try different varieties until you find what suits your particular needs.

WINTER RADISHES (*Raphanus sativus*)—These radishes are slower in growth, much larger, and longer keeping than spring types. They are almost always grown as a fall crop because the decreasing temperatures and day length discourage flowering.

When planted in spring, most varieties flower before sizable roots can develop. An exception is All Season, a long white variety of the Japanese "daikon" type. Well grown daikons are smooth, cylindrical, and up to 18 inches in length while still of excellent quality.

A giant beet-shaped variety, Sakurajima, can reach 50 pounds or more if a long fall growing period is available. Smaller varieties such as Long Black Spanish and Chinese Rose Winter are also available.

Try varieties to find the degrees of pungency desired. Depending on conditions, they vary from very hot to mild. Winter radishes retain good texture for a long period and are good for cooking and pickling as well as fresh table use.

TURNIP (*Brassica rapa*)—The turnip is second to spring radish in quick growth and short life. In hot weather the roots are often strong or bitter in flavor and become pithy almost when they reach maximum size. For this reason turnips are usually grown for harvest in spring and fall and sometimes planted several times during each of these seasons. Cabbage root maggot control is the most critical culture problem.

One variety, Purple Top White Globe, dominates home garden turnip production. There are other choices, however, including pure white, yellow, and red varieties if catalogs are searched. Special varieties for greens such as Shogoin are available, but the tops of any variety can be used.

RUTABAGA (*Brassica campestris* var. *napobrassica*)—Originating long ago from a cross between cabbage and turnip, rutabaga generally resembles turnip but has slower growth, longer storage life, less prickly leaves, firmer flesh, and a great deal more vitamin A.

Rutabagas may be left in the ground for use during winter, if climate permits, or stored for long periods. They do not become pithy if overmature, as turnips do. Cabbage root maggot control is equally critical, however.

Most rutabagas grown are of the variety American Purple Top. Others encountered, such as Laurentian, are essentially the same or of no better quality.

Greens or "Potherbs"—Chard, Collards, Kale, Mustard, Spinach, New Zealand Spinach

by Albert A. Banadyga

Greens include chard, collards, kale, mustard, spinach, and New Zealand spinach. Grown for their tender and succulent leaves and stems, greens are often referred to as "potherbs" since they are usually cooked before eating.

Quite easy to grow, greens require a relatively short growing season. Greens are good sources of some of the vitamins and minerals. They are tasty when cooked fresh from the garden. Raw greens are often added to tossed salads to give them additional color and a different and zestful flavor.

Greens are cool season crops, with the exception of New Zealand spinach. Thus home gardeners normally plant and grow them during cooler periods of the year—spring and fall.

Rapid and continuous growth is essential for both high quality and high yields. To obtain this growth, you need to provide a fairly rich soil containing adequate amounts of organic matter, a good supply of plant nutrients, and a continuous supply of soil moisture.

CHARD (*Beta vulgaris* var. *cicla*)— often called Swiss chard, is a type of beet developed for its large crisp leaves and fleshy leafstalks rather than its roots. It is of quite ancient origin, first reported in the Mediterranean region and the Canary Islands.

Chard is a popular garden vegetable, particularly in the North. It will withstand warm summer temperatures, so that a planting in the early spring can be continuously harvested throughout the summer and fall.

One serving of cooked chard has

Albert A. Banadyga is Extension Horticulturist, North Carolina State University, Raleigh.

13 calories and provides 87% of the Vitamin A and 25% of the Vitamin C required daily by the average adult.

Chard thrives best in a well-drained mellow or friable (crumbly) soil, such as a sandy or clay loam. However, it will grow well in most soils if provided with nutrients and moisture. Soil pH may range from 6.0 to 6.8. Chard is a cool season crop, will withstand light frosts, and does best if planted in the early spring about 2 to 4 weeks before the last frost.

The optimum monthly average temperature for plant growth is 60° to 65° F with a monthly minimum average of 40° and a monthly maximum average of 75°. Soil temperatures for seed germination may range from 50° to 85° with a minimum of 40°, an optimum of 85° and a maximum of 95°.

Adequate soil moisture is especially important for seed germination and early plant growth. Irrigation is particularly beneficial during dry conditions.

Popular varieties include Lucullus, Fordhook Giant, Large White Rib, and Rhubarb (red stemmed). Chard has a multiple seed, as does the beet. Thus one to six plants may emerge from each seed. There are about 1,200 seeds per ounce.

Fertilizing

Before planting, broadcast about 3 pints of a complete fertilizer, such as 10-10-10, to each 50 feet of row. Mix the fertilizer thoroughly with the upper 6 to 8 inches of soil. The seed bed should be thoroughly prepared, free of clods and trash, and slightly firmed.

Distance between rows may be 18 inches. Make a slight furrow in the row, about ½ inch deep, and plant the seeds in the furrow 1 to 2 inches apart. Cover the seed with ½ inch of soil and firm lightly with the back of a rake. Seedlings should emerge in 8 to 10 days.

As the plants grow, periodically thin them out until they are about 12 inches apart. Plants pulled out in the thinning process may be used as greens.

For a very early crop, plants may be started in a greenhouse or cold-frame and transplanted to the garden after danger of heavy frosts is over. Plant the seeds in cups, or other small containers, about 3 to 4 weeks before they are to be planted in the open garden. Be sure to "harden-off" the tender plants by gradually withholding water and exposing them to outside weather conditions. Hardening-off should begin about a week before the plants are set out in the open.

Control weeds by hoeing before the weeds get a good start. Or better still, mulch the young plants with such materials as straw, grass clippings, newspapers, or black plastic film.

Be on the lookout for such insects as cabbage worms, aphids, beet leaf miner, and flea beetle. Worms may

Left, Fordhook Giant Swiss chard. Right, Swiss chard, properly spaced and with outer leaves ready for harvest. These average about a foot high, and should not be left to become coarse and over-grown.

be removed by hand picking, aphids may be washed off with a fine spray of water from a garden hose, or recommended insecticides may be used. Crop rotation and sanitation will help reduce damage from leaf spots and other diseases.

For rapid and continuous growth, sidedress the crop about a month after planting. Repeat at 4- to 6-week intervals. At each sidedressing uniformily distribute one pint of a complete fertilizer (or one cup of sodium nitrate) per 50 feet of row. Place the fertilizer in a band 4 to 6 inches out to the side of the plants, making certain not to get any on the plants themselves.

Leaves and stems are ready for harvest about 50 to 60 days after planting. With a sharp knife cut off a few of the outer leaves, about an inch above ground, while they are still tender and succulent. Cut carefully to

avoid injury to younger leaves and the central bud. Continue harvesting throughout the summer and fall. As you remove the outer stems and leaves, new ones will continue to form and grow from the central bud.

Harvesting should be continued, regardless of whether or not the greens will be used, or else new leaves will not be available later in the season.

A good yield, for the full season, is about one pound of chard greens per foot of row. A 30-foot row will supply an average family of 4 with an adequate supply of fresh chard greens throughout the season.

Some gardeners dig up the plants just before the first heavy freeze in fall, and store the entire plant in a protected cellar or coldframe for continued harvest into the winter. Plants are stacked upright, with roots in contact with the soil, and watered lightly to prevent excessive wilting and to encourage a very limited amount of continued growth.

COLLARDS (*Brassica oleraceae* var. *acephala*)—originated in the British Isles and Western Europe. The collard is often called a non-heading cabbage, since it does not form a true head but rather a large rosette of leaves. It belongs to the cabbage family and its culture and use are quite similar to those of cabbage. It may be grown throughout the year in the South, and as both a spring and fall crop in the North.

One serving of cooked collards has 21 calories and provides 87% of the Vitamin A, 74% of the Vitamin C, and 14% of the calcium in the minimum daily requirements of an average adult.

Collards may be grown on a very wide range of soils, but sandy, silt, or clay loams are preferred. Soil pH may range between 5.5 to 6.8, with 6.0 being ideal. The plant is a heavy feeder, often growing to a height of 3 to 4 feet.

Optimum monthly average temperatures for plant growth are 60° to 65° F with a monthly minimum average of 40° and a monthly maximum average of 75°. Soil temperature for seed germination may range from 45° to 95° with a minimum of 40°, an optimum of 85° and a maximum of 100°. Collards will withstand a greater range of temperature, both heat and cold, than most other vegetables grown in the South. If the temperature drops gradually over a period of several days, collards can withstand temperatures as low as 15°.

Collard seed will germinate in 4 to 9 days even under low soil moisture conditions. The plants grow best in well-drained soils that are provided with adequate moisture by rainfall or irrigation.

Popular Varieties

Vates, Morris Heading, Georgia, Cabbage-Collard, and Green Glaze are popular varieties. One-fourth ounce of seed is sufficient to plant 100 feet of row. There are about 8,000 seeds per ounce.

Collards are hardy and may be planted in the spring about 4 to 6 weeks before the last spring frost and again in the fall about 6 to 8 weeks before the first fall frost. Prepare the soil as suggested for chard. Broadcast 4 pints of fertilizer, such as 10-10-10, per 50 feet of row and mix it thoroughly with the soil before planting. Rows are normally 3 to 4 feet apart.

Collards may be seeded directly in the garden or transplanted. When seeding directly in the garden, plant the seed ¼-inch deep and about 1 inch apart in the row. Seedlings will emerge in about 5 days. Plants may be left at the seeded spacing, or thinned to 6, 12, or 18 inches apart depending on how they will be harvested. The plants pulled out in thinning may serve as transplants or trimmed and used as greens.

245-559 O - '77 - 5

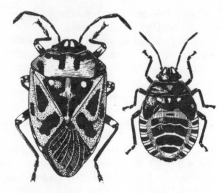

Harlequin bug. Adult, left. Nymph, right.

Transplants may be grown in protected beds in the spring and in open plant beds in the summer. Seeds are planted in individual containers, flats, or rows in ground beds about 4 to 6 weeks before time to transplant into the garden. When plants are 6 to 8 inches tall, set them in the garden row 12 to 18 inches apart, and water well.

About a month after planting in the garden, sidedress collards as suggested for chard.

Control weeds by hoeing or mulching. Insects that may cause problems include cabbage worms, aphids, harlequin bugs, and root maggots. Two diseases that may cause damage are downy mildew and black leg. General control measures are the same as suggested previously for chard.

Collards may be harvested by three general methods, or a combination of the three. The entire young plant may be cut off at ground level just as are mustard greens, the entire mature plant may be cut off at the ground, or the bottom leaves may be stripped off the plant periodically leaving the bud to grow and produce more leaves. The last method is most popular with home gardeners since it entails making only one planting, and spring-planted collards may be continuously harvested throughout the summer and into winter.

When the entire small or immature plants are to be harvested, successive plantings may be made at 2- to 3-week intervals. Immature plants may be harvested about 40 days and mature plants about 75 days after planting.

Collards tend to improve in flavor as the weather becomes cooler in the fall. Many gardeners do not harvest the fall crop until after the first frost. Leaves remain tender and edible for several weeks after they reach maturity or full size.

Yields vary from ⅓ to 1½ pounds per foot of row, depending on harvesting methods used.

KALE (*Brassica oleraceae* var. *acephala*)—is a native of Europe and recorded use dates back to 200 B.C. Like collards, it is a member of the cabbage family and is grown for its succulent leaves and stems.

A hardy vegetable, kale can be overwintered in latitudes as far north as southern Pennsylvania and in areas having similar winter conditions. It is also quite heat-resistant and may grow in the summer, but its greatest value is as a cool weather green. No other vegetable is so well adapted to fall sowing in areas having winters of moderate severity.

One serving of cooked kale has 21 calories. It provides an average adult with all his daily requirements of Vitamin A and Vitamin C as well as 13% of his daily calcium requirement.

Temperature, soil, fertility, and moisture conditions for kale are the same as previously suggested for collards.

Vates, Dwarf Siberian, and Dwarf Blue Scotch are good standard varieties. Seed may be planted in the spring 4 to 6 weeks before the last killing frost, and in the fall 6 to 8 weeks before the first killing frost. There are about 10,000 seeds per ounce.

Rows may be 18 to 24 inches apart.

Seed is planted in the row an inch apart and a half inch deep. Seedlings will emerge in 3 to 5 days. Plants may be left as thick as seeded or gradually thinned until they are 8 to 14 inches apart. The plants pulled out in thinning may be used as greens.

Pests and pest control for kale are similar to those suggested previously for collards.

Kale may be harvested in one of two ways. The entire young plants may be cut off at ground level, about 40 days after seeding. This process is used when the plants are left unthinned after seeding.

When plants are spaced 8 to 14 inches apart, the lower leaves are stripped off periodically while the bud and a rosette of leaves are left to continue growth for future harvests. This second harvest method requires about 50 to 60 days from seeding to first harvest. Leaves should be harvested before they become old, tough, and woody.

A foot of row will produce about a half pound of kale greens.

MUSTARD (Brassica juncea var. crispifolia)—also known as "mustard greens," is a short season crop grown for its tender leaves and stems. This crop had its origin in China and Asia. A different species, black mustard, is grown for its dark seed which is used in making the condiment known as table mustard.

One serving of cooked mustard greens has 16 calories and provides 91% of the Vitamin A, 74% of the Vitamin C, and 12% of the calcium in the daily requirements of an average adult.

Soil, fertility, and moisture requirements for mustard greens are similar to those previously suggested for collards. This crop will not withstand the extremes in temperature that kale

Top, collards are a nutritious crop found in many gardens of Southeastern U.S. Left, collard plant ready for harvest.

and collards will. It also bolts (goes to seed) much more rapidly, particularly in spring.

Optimum monthly average temperature for plant growth is 60° to 65° F with a monthly minimum average of 45° and a monthly maximum average of 70° to 75°. Optimum soil temperature range for seed germination is 60° to 105° with a minimum of 40°, an optimum of 85°, and a maximum of 105°.

Reliable mustard varieties include Southern Giant Curled, Tendergreen, Florida Broadleaf, and Green Wave. One-fourth ounce of seed will plant 100 feet of row. There are about 15,000 seeds per ounce.

Soil preparation and fertilization are similar to those previously suggested for collards. Seeds are planted directly in the row about 4 to 6 weeks before the last frost in the spring and about 6 to 8 weeks before the first frost in the fall. Additional successive plantings may be made at two-week intervals. Rows may be 15 to 30 inches apart. Seeds are planted in the row, an inch apart and ¼ inch deep. Seedlings will emerge in 3 to 5 days.

Plants may be left unthinned or thinned to 4 to 6 inches apart. The plants thinned out may be used for greens.

Pests and pest control are the same as described for collards.

The young tender leaves are harvested any time after they reach 6 to 8 inches in height and before they become tough and woody. Harvest begins about 35 to 40 days after seeding. Normally the entire plant is cut off slightly above the ground. In the Deep South, mustard greens may be carried over into winter and harvested by stripping the lower leaves similar to collards and kale.

One foot of row will yield about a half pound of mustard greens.

SPINACH (*Spinacia oleraceae* var. *inermis*)—was cultivated by the Persians over 2,000 years ago. The edible

Below, rows of spinach in a garden. Bottom, Long Standing Bloomsdale spinach.

portion of the plant is the compact rosette of leaves before the central bud begins to elongate to form a seedstalk.

This is a hardy cool weather crop. In most of the United States it is grown as an early spring and a late fall crop. In some areas having mild summer temperatures, spinach is grown continuously from early spring to late fall. In portions of the South it may be planted in the fall and harvested during the winter and early spring.

A serving of cooked spinach has 20 calories. It provides an average adult with 100% of the Vitamin A, 56% of the Vitamin C, and 28% of the iron indicated in the minimum daily requirement.

Spinach will grow on almost any fertile soil that is well drained and has a good supply of organic matter. Avoid poorly drained soils or those that cake or crust easily. The soil pH range is 6.0 to 6.8. Spinach grows poorly on soils with a pH below 6.0.

Optimum monthly average temperature for plant growth is 60° to 65° F. Optimum monthly minimum average is 40° and optimum maximum average is 75°. Optimum soil temperature for seed germination is 70° with a minimum of 35° and a maximum of 85°.

Spinach is shallow rooted; provide adequate soil moisture for rapid and continuous growth.

Among the leading spinach varieties for fall production are Hybrid #7, Virginia Savoy, Resistoflay, Viroflay, and Chesapeake. Among the better spring varieties are Long Standing Bloomsdale and America. A half ounce of seed will plant 100 feet of row. There are approximately 2,800 seeds per ounce.

Spinach is normally planted about 4 to 6 weeks before the last frost in the spring and again 6 to 8 weeks before the first frost in fall. Two to three successive plantings may be made at 2- to 3- week intervals.

Rows are usually 14 to 30 inches apart, depending on cultivation equipment to be used. Before planting, broadcast about 3 to 4 pints of fertilizer, such as 10-10-10, per 50 feet of row and mix thoroughly with the soil. Plant seeds in the row a half inch deep and an inch apart. It takes spinach seedlings about 5 to 8 days to emerge. Thin plants to a 3- to 4-inch spacing before they become crowded in the row.

Keep weeds out by hoeing before they get a good start. Use varieties resistant to mildew and yellows. Observe plants closely for aphids, leaf miners, or cabbage worms. Use similar control measures as suggested under chard.

Spinach may be harvested from the time the plants have 5 to 6 leaves until just before seedstalks develop. This period is usually 35 to 45 days after seeding. Harvest by cutting the entire plant off, just above ground level, with a sharp knife.

One foot of row will yield a third to a half pound of spinach greens.

NEW ZEALAND SPINACH (*Tetragonia expansa*)—is a native of New Zealand, Japan, Australia, and South America. It was introduced to England in 1771 and is presently grown to a very limited extent in the United States. Not a true spinach, it does resemble spinach somewhat in appearance and is used similarly.

The plant is large, growing to a height of two or more feet in a spreading and branching habit of growth, and has thick succulent leaves. It is a warm season crop and an excellent source of fresh greens throughout the summer.

One serving of cooked New Zealand spinach has 11 calories and provides 72% of the Vitamin A, 27% of the Vitamin C, and 10% of the iron in an average adult's minimum daily requirement.

New Zealand spinach thrives in a well drained loamy soil, high in organic matter and fertility. A soil pH of 6.0 to 6.8 is desirable. Fertility and soil moisture needs are similar to those for spinach. The plant grows best with a monthly average temperature of 60° to 75° F, a monthly minimum average of 50° and a monthly maximum average of 95°. Optimum soil temperature range for seed germination is 70° to 95° with a minimum of 60° and a maximum of 100°.

Since this is a warm season crop,

New Zealand spinach.

delay planting until danger of spring frosts is over and the soil has warmed.

Space rows 3 to 4 feet apart. Before planting, broadcast 3 pints of fertilizer, such as 10-10-10, per 50 feet of row and mix thoroughly with the soil.

Seed is large and irregularly shaped with a count of about 350 per ounce. Plant seeds in the row 1 inch deep and 4 to 6 inches apart. To insure prompt germination, soak seed in warm water for 2 to 3 hours before planting.

Seedlings normally emerge in 7 to 12 days. Plants may be gradually thinned out until they are spaced 12 to 18 inches apart in the row.

Control weeds by hoeing or with a mulch. There are no insects or diseases of consequence.

About 4 to 6 weeks after planting, sidedress with either one pint of fertilizer (such as 10-10-10) or ½ cup of nitrate of soda per 50 feet of row.

Harvest may begin about 70 days after seeding. Successive harvests of the tips are made from a single planting. At each harvest about 3 inches of the tips of the branches are cut or pinched off. This results in more branching and more new succulent growth. The thick leaves as well as the tender stems are cooked.

Harvesting continues throughout the summer and until the first fall frost. Take care not to remove too large a portion of the plant at one time. During early harvests, a half to two-thirds of the branch tips may be taken at one harvest. As the plant continues to branch a greater portion of the tips may be harvested at one time.

One foot of row will yield about three-fourths pound of greens for the entire season.

Summary: Greens are easy to grow and quite nutritious. For maximum yields and quality, growth should be rapid and continuous. To insure such growth, provide for a well drained soil, add organic matter if needed to keep the soil loamy and retentive of moisure and nutrients, maintain an adequate fertilizer level, provide for adequate moisture, plant during the proper season, control pests, and harvest at peak of quality.

Beans and Peas Are Easy to Grow And Produce a Wealth of Food

by Jack P. Meiners and John M. Kraft

Beans and peas are among the most satisfying vegetables for home garden growing and eating. The seeds are planted directly in the garden, and germinate rapidly to give rise to plants that grow quickly and vigorously. This gives even the beginning gardener a feeling of accomplishment. In fact, beans and peas should be in every garden because they are easy to grow and provide a wealth of food.

When we speak merely of beans and peas we are over-simplifying the situation regarding legumes of interest to the home gardener. Actually, he can choose from several types of legumes, all of which make tasty and highly nutritious food for the family. Beans may include snap or string beans, dry beans, and lima beans. Peas include garden pea—also called English pea—and southernpea, also known as cowpea.

Beans and peas are discussed together in this section because, botanically speaking, they are related. Both are members of the legume family, which bear the characteristic butterfly-like flowers and have the capacity with the help of bacteria in the root nodules to take nitrogen out of the air. Otherwise, beans and peas differ from each other somewhat in culture. Most beans and southernpea are warm weather plants while garden pea requires cool growing conditions.

Snap Beans

Snap bean is one of several types

J. P. Meiners is Chief, Applied Plant Pathology Laboratory, Agricultural Research Center, Beltsville, Md. John M. Kraft is Research Plant Pathologist, Agricultural Research Service, Irrigated Agriculture Research and Extension Center, Prosser, Wash.

of bean known collectively as "common bean" and by the scientific name, *Phaseolus vulgaris*. The home gardener may grow several kinds depending upon how he plans to use the product.

Those grown for the immature pods are known variously as "snap" beans, "string" beans, "green" beans, "French" beans, or "garden" beans. Other types grown for the immature seeds are known as "green shell" beans, and still others grown for the mature seeds are called "dry" beans. All the types are similar in requirements for growing in the garden.

Snap beans, used when the pods are immature, need only a short growing season and thus are favored by most home gardeners.

The common bean probably originated in Central America, but has been cultivated throughout much of North and South America by the Indians since prehistoric times. Because the seeds were easily carried and stored, and because beans grew well in a variety of climates, they were widely distributed by the explorers and now are widely grown throughout the world.

The Indians probably consumed beans primarily in the dry or green shell state, and early varieties of snap beans were stringy—hence the term "string" beans. The tender, stringless and nearly fiberless varieties we know today were developed within the last 50 years.

Snap beans are a good source of vitamins A and C, thiamine, and riboflavin. They are also a good source of calcium and iron.

Snap beans are a warm season crop and easily injured by frost. The first of several successive plantings should be made at about the time of the aver-

range of soils, the best being those that are well drained and reasonably fertile. The physical nature of the soil should be friable and not interfere with emergence. Upon germination, the two large seed halves or cotyledons must emerge through the soil and they can be seriously hampered by compact or crusted soil.

If your soil is very heavy you may need to cover the seed with sand, peat, leaf mulch, or other material that will not form a crust. Should a crust form following planting, it may be necessary to break it to allow the seedlings to emerge from the soil. If you live in an area of heavy rainfall you may need to plant beans on raised beds to get proper drainage.

Snap beans are not heavy users of water but require a constant supply. One inch per week is sufficient on most types of soils. An adequate supply of moisture is important from bud formation to pod set. Excessive or too little moisture may cause blossom and pod drop. If soil is too dry at planting time, it is preferable to irrigate first, then plant.

age frost-free date for your area. Usually there is not much to be gained by planting earlier, since early planted beans require longer to mature and there is the risk that seed may rot in the cold soil, with additional delay if reseeding becomes necessary.

Snap beans grow best where the average maximum temperature does not exceed 85° F and the average minimum temperature does not go below 50°, but the most desirable range is between 70° and 80°. Very high temperatures lower the yield due to blossom drop.

The soil should be warm at planting time. Snap bean seed germinates poorly at soil temperatures below 50° F and the optimum range is between 60° and 85°.

In the lower South and Southwest, snap beans may be grown during all seasons except mid-winter, but should not be planted so that podding occurs when weather is too hot or cold.

Snap beans grow well in a wide

Bush and Pole

There are two basic plant habits—bush and pole. The bush is a low, self-supporting plant that grows 1 to 2 feet in height. Pole beans are vines which must be supported by stakes or a trellis.

Use bush varieties for quick production and pole types for a longer season. Successive plantings of bush types every 10 to 14 days will provide beans for most of the growing season. Because pole beans bear over a longer period, usually one planting suffices.

Disease-free Western-grown seed should be used rather than that grown by the gardener since snap beans are

Tendercrop snap bean is mosaic-resistant and heavy yielding. It has tender, round, green pods and wide range of adaptability.

Planting Guide for Beans and Peas

Type	Pounds of seed per 50-ft row	Depth of planting, inches	Spacing between rows, inches	Spacing in rows, inches		Days to harvest
				Seeds	Plants	
Snap beans, bush	¼–½	1–1½	18–30	1–2	2–4	50–60
Snap beans, pole	¼–½	1–1½	24–48	3–6	4–8	60–70
Lima beans, bush	¼–½	1–1½	18–30	2–4	4–8	65–75
Lima beans, pole	¼–½	1–1½	36	3–6	6–8	70–90
Peas, garden	¼	1–2	6 (double rows) 36–48	1–1½	1–1½	55–70
Peas, southern	¼–½	1–1½	30–54	2–4	2–4	55–80

Don Normark

subject to diseases carried on the seed. Do not soak the seed prior to planting because seeds of many bean varieties tend to crack and germinate poorly under extreme moisture conditions.

Bush-type beans are most commonly planted in rows 18 to 30 inches apart with seeds placed 1 to 2 inches apart and thinned so plants are 2 to 4 inches apart.

Pole beans may also be planted in rows 2 to 4 feet apart with vines supported by poles, a fence, or a trellis made of posts and twine. In addition, they may be planted in hills about 3 feet apart each way, with 6 to 8 seeds in each hill, and later thinned to 4 to 5 plants. A pole is placed in the center of every hill with each pole upright, or four poles are tied together in wigwam fashion. Gardeners usually train the vines to climb the supports in a clockwise direction.

Bean seed should be covered not more than 1 inch in heavy soils and 1½ inches in sandy soils.

If the vegetable garden has received a general application of manure, com-

Corn may get as high as an elephant's eye, but pole beans can top that when properly trellised.

173

post, or commercial fertilizer, beans should need no additional fertilizer during the growing season. Where no fertilizer has been applied, a moderate application of one such as 5-10-5 usually is all you need. Avoid heavy applications of fertilizers high in nitrogen as they may cause heavy vine growth, delayed maturity, and a small yield of pods.

On light soils or after periods of heavy rainfall, you may need to side-dress the plants with a nitrogenous fertilizer during the growing season.

Mulching of beans with organic materials or black plastic is recommended since it conserves moisture and prevents weed growth. Black plastic also hastens early season growth.

Control weeds by cultivating or hoeing. These operations should be very shallow since bean roots are close to the surface. In cultivating, throw soil against the bean stems to aid in support and development of additional roots. An adequate mulch greatly decreases weed growth.

Pest Control

Snap beans suffer from diseases and insect pests, the number and intensity of attack depending upon geographic location. In the West, virus diseases and root rots are the most serious diseases. In the East and South, bacterial and fungus leaf and pod diseases are most important.

Diseases are best controlled by preventative measures such as using disease-free, Western-grown seed which controls bacterial diseases and anthracnose; planting disease-resistant varieties when available which controls virus diseases and rust; and using seed treated with pesticide to control soil-borne diseases and insects.

Practicing cleanliness and sanitation in the garden controls many diseases and insects. Not handling or working among the bean plants when the foliage is wet from dew or rain helps control bacterial diseases. Not planting beans in the same ground year after year reduces root rots.

Seed catalogs or State agricultural experiment station publications usually indicate if varieties are resistant to particular diseases.

Insects must be controlled with insecticides applied to the plants (for aphids, Mexican bean beetle, mites, potato leafhopper), or seed (for the seed corn maggot). Contact your local county agent or State university for specific control recommendations.

Snap beans are best for eating while the pods are still young, the seeds still small, the interior flesh is firm, and the pod wall fiber content low. The proper stage for picking lasts only a few days and delay can mean a poor quality product.

Bush varieties usually yield three or four pickings whereas pole varieties yield numerous pickings. Regular and thorough picking of both types is important because it causes the plants to continue to set pods longer.

Yields can vary tremendously, but bush beans yield about 50 pounds per hundred feet of row and pole beans about 60 pounds.

Green shell beans are harvested and shelled out after the seeds are nearly fully grown, but before they have hardened and dried. Snap bean varieties may be used for green shell beans, but it is better to plant one of the horticultural varieties for this purpose. Depending on variety, from planting to green shell stage will take 55 to 75 days.

Dry beans are harvested after the pods are mature and dried or partially dried. Delay in harvesting may result in loss of seed due to shattering.

Lima Beans

Natives of the Western Hemisphere, limas probably originated in Central America. The small seeded types have been cultivated since prehistoric times in North America. The large seeded

Below, Fordhook 242 bush lima beans are vigorous, productive and heat-resistant. Right, trellised lima beans. Bottom, lima pole beans growing on strings.

Terence O Driscoll

types were developed in South America, specifically in Peru, hence the name "lima" from the capital city of that country.

The growing of lima beans is similar to that of snap beans. Therefore, this section will emphasize mainly the cultural requirements specific for limas, and we suggest that the prospective lima bean grower read the section on growing snap beans also.

Lima beans fall into two classes as far as the gardener is concerned—the large seeded, generally referred to as Fordhook type, and the small seeded, known as baby limas. The scientific name for both types is *Phaseolus lunatus*. In the South the lima is called butter bean.

Both large and small seeded limas come in bush or pole types similar to those of snap beans.

Lima beans are used as green shell beans when the seeds have developed to nearly full size. The pods are not consumed. Nutritionally, lima beans are high in the vitamins thiamine and riboflavin and in phosphorus and iron.

Lima beans require warmer soil and air temperatures than snap beans, and thus are planted somewhat later. A planting date of 2 weeks after the average date of the last frost probably is a good rule-of-thumb. Furthermore, lima beans need a frost-free period of 3 to 4 months with relatively warm days and nights.

Proper soil temperature is critical for seed germination and should be 65° F for quick emergence of seedlings.

Gardeners in most of the more northerly parts of the United States, including the northern New England States and parts of other States along the Canadian border, probably should not attempt to grow lima beans. Just south of this region only bush baby limas should be grown since they mature in a shorter period than large seeded bush or pole limas.

Lima beans grow best in lighter-textured, well-drained soils. They need a soil somewhat richer than required for snap beans, but not excessive in nitrogen.

Don't plant lima beans until two or more weeks after snap beans are first planted. To lengthen the growing season, plant protectors can be used over the seeds and young plants in marginal areas—or to obtain earlier growth in other regions. It is possible also for gardeners to start limas indoors and transplant to the garden. Be sure the root systems are not disturbed in transplanting.

Because of requirements for a longer growing season, successive plantings of bush lima beans should not be made except in the more southern areas of the United States.

Seed Treatment Vital

If at all possible, lima bean seed should be treated with a fungicide and insecticide before planting, especially if the soil temperature is below 65° F. Consult your seedsman, county agent, or State university as to the proper seed treatment and follow the label instructions carefully.

Lima beans may be attacked by a number of diseases and insects. Many of these pests also attack snap beans. As mentioned previously, lima beans are more subject to seed and seedling diseases, so seed treatment is essential to obtaining good stands and sturdy plants.

In the Mid-Atlantic States mildew may be a problem and can be controlled by fungicides or use of resistant varieties, if available. In the South anthracnose may be serious and should be controlled with a fungicide. Nematodes may be a problem, particularly in the South. These can be controlled through resistant varieties and soil fumigation.

Insect control through insecticides may be necessary.

Consult your county agent or State university for diagnosis and recommendation of specific control measures against pests.

Lima beans are ready for picking when the pods are well filled but still bright and fresh in appearance. The end of the pod should feel spongy when squeezed.

Bush limas can be picked for about 3 weeks and pole limas for about 4 weeks or until frost. Depending upon soil fertility, temperature, moisture, and many other factors, yields of from 20 to 40 pounds per 100 feet of row may be expected.

Garden Peas

The garden pea (*Pisum sativum* L.) is thought to have originated in Eastern Europe or Western Asia and was widely distributed in prehistoric times. It has been traced back to the stone age where dried seeds were found among relics of the Swiss Lake villages.

However, the eating of green peas was not referred to until the Norman conquest around 1066.

Green pea consumption was not common until the 18th century but with the appearance of canning and freezing, peas have become an important vegetable crop. To distinguish them from the field pea, used dried and split, or the southernpea, garden peas are often called green peas or English peas.

Peas are a cool weather, rapid maturing crop. They must be planted early for maximum yield and should be brought to maturity under cool conditions.

The garden pea thrives best when grown in the South and lower parts of California during fall, winter and early spring. Farther North, peas thrive when grown in spring or autumn. In the Northern States and at higher elevations, they may be grown from spring until autumn; however, if summer heat is too severe, the season may be limited to spring.

Sandy or rocky soils usually result in early crops, but plants on these soil types frequently suffer from water stress if there is no supplemental irrigation.

Select a seed bed site which is uniform, level and well drained. The seed bed should be worked at least to a depth of about 2½ inches. A well prepared seed bed is essential for uniform germination and seedling stands. Peas will not thrive on poorly drained or water soaked land.

An adequate range in soil pH for peas is between 5.5 and 6.7. A soil with excessive organic residue or nitrogen is not ideal for pea growth because it promotes rank vine growth at the expense of pod production.

Peas are usually planted from 1 to 1½ inches deep (heavy soils) to 2 inches deep (sandy soils) as soon as the soil can be properly worked. Peas are sown 8 or 10 to the foot.

The seed should be treated with a commercial seed protectant and planted in single or double rows. The double rows should be about 6 inches apart which allows dwarf or bush varieties to cling and hold one another up. When planted in single rows, the dwarf varieties should be sown in rows 3 feet apart and the taller varieties 4 feet apart.

If the plants are to be supported, wire netting or string trellis can be put between the rows. Tall varieties usually do better when grown on a trellis. However, left unsupported they will form a ground cover, smothering the weeds.

Staked or trellised plants will usually require some hand weeding. Always avoid deep hoeing that may injure the roots.

Peas have a number of disease and insect pests. Preventive measures are desirable—for example, protective seed treatments, never plant peas in the same location in succession, and remove old vines from the garden.

If a disease or insect problem appears that you aren't familiar with,

Picking and sampling green peas.

consult your county agent. And keep in mind the many excellent books and articles available from public libraries and garden stores, as well as the extension bulletins on vegetable gardening and pest control.

In general, harvest the pods when they appear well filled but before they begin to harden or fade in color.

Peas will yield the maximum food value when the seeds are full size. A few days before this stage, however, peas are at their prime for taste and tenderness.

The number of pickings will be at least two or three, since pea pods do not all mature at the same time but usually during a period of 7 to 10 days.

Pull the pods carefully off the vine, or plants may be uprooted. For best quality, pick peas just before meal preparation or processing because sugar conversion to starch will begin only a few hours after picking.

Edible podded peas (sugar peas, Chinese peas, snow peas) have pod walls that are tender, brittle, succulent, and free from fiber. After destringing, the young pods are cooked whole (like snap beans), or used as greens in salads. If pods develop too fast, eat the shelled peas.

Southernpeas

In the South the unqualified word "pea" usually refers to the southernpea, also known as cowpea and protopea. There are several distinct types of southern pea of which blackeye, crowder, and cream are the best known. Each of these types has its own unique appearance and flavor.

Southernpeas (*Vigna unguiculata*) are highly nutritious, tasty, and easily grown. They deserve to be much more widely grown by home gardeners.

Southernpeas are natives of Africa, brought to the West Indies by slave traders. From there they are believed

Terence O'Driscoll

to have been introduced to the United States in the 1700's. Southernpeas are consumed as fresh shelled peas, sometimes mixed with the immature pods, and as dry peas. Nutritionally, they are similar to lima beans.

The yard-long bean, or asparagus bean, a pole type of cowpea, produces pods 1 to 2 feet long. However, it is less productive than other varieties, and commonly used in Chinese cookery.

The southernpea is a warm weather crop and should be planted much later in the spring than snap beans. Adequate stands are difficult to achieve until the soil is quite warm. Although well suited to summer culture in the South, it also is adapted to northern conditions of about the same range as the lima bean.

Southernpeas are adapted to a wide range of climatic, soil and cultural conditions and are particularly drought and heat tolerant. Excess moisture causes reduction in yield.

As with beans, southernpeas may be classified as vining, semi-vining, or bush types. Also, there are short-, mid-, and long-season varieties. The bush or compact varieties that mature quickly are most suitable for home gardening, particularly outside the deep South. Southernpeas are usually planted in rows 2½ to 3½ feet apart with an inter-row spacing between seeds of 2 to 4 inches.

Heavy applications of nitrogen fertilizers should not be used for southernpeas. An application of a low nitrogen fertilizer such as 4-12-12 applied at the equivalent of 1½ to 2½ pounds per 50 feet of row usually is adequate.

Seed should be purchased from a seedsman as it is more apt to be free of disease and true to variety than if the gardener saves his own seed. If possible, the seed should be treated with a fungicide and insecticide.

Planting southernpeas.

In the South, successive plantings made about three weeks apart until mid-summer will give a continuous supply of green peas.

Various insects and diseases attack southernpeas. Some can destroy the crop while others do little damage.

The most destructive insect, especially in the South, is the cowpea curculio which feeds on the pods and seeds as they develop. Other insects also may be destructive to the plant and several species of weevils may seriously damage stored cowpea seed.

Application of insecticides is essential for successful culture of southernpeas in the South, especially during the fall. Several insects, such as the southern green stinkbug and cornworm, cause great damage during this time of year.

Specific information on insecticide application may be obtained from your county agent or State agricultural experiment station.

Diseases include wilt, root knot, and those caused by viruses. They may be best controlled by use of resistant varieties, planting disease free and treated seed, removing old vines, and not planting peas in the same location in successive years.

Southernpeas for home use as fresh-shelled peas are harvested when the deep green pod color changes—depending upon specific variety—to light yellow, silver, red or purple. The peas should be almost maximum in size but with appreciable green color still in the cotyledon.

A rule-of-thumb states that peas should be harvested 16 days after bloom, but this depends on the temperature. Depending on variety and environmental conditions, peas may be ready for picking from 55 to 80 days after planting.

For Further Reading:

Grow Your Own Green Beans, Extension Service, Ext. Cir. 886, Industrial Bldg., Oregon State University, Corvallis, Oreg. 97331. 5¢

Grow Your Own Vegetables, Cooperative Extension Service, Ext. Cir. 559, Pennsylvania State University, University Park, Pa. 16802. 10¢

Growing Vegetables in the Home Garden, H. and G. Bul. 202, for sale by Superintendent of Documents, U.S. Government Printing Office, Washington, D.C. 20402. 95¢

Home and Farm Vegetable Garden, Ext. Cir. 871, Extension Service, Industrial Bldg., Oregon State University, Corvallis, Oreg. 97331. 15¢

Home Gardens, Cooperative Extension Service, Ext. Cir. 442, Washington State University, Pullman, Wash. 99163. 20¢

Home Vegetable Gardening, Cooperative Extension Service, Ext. Cir. 457, New Mexico State University, Las Cruces, N. M. 88003. Free

Illinois Vegetable Garden Guide, Cooperative Extension Service, Ext. Cir. 1091, University of Illinois, Champaign-Urbana, Ill. 61801.

More Vegetables From Your Garden, Extension Division, Pub. 657, Virginia Polytechnic Institute and State University, Blacksburg, Va. 24061. 12¢

Plant Diseases, Cooperative Extension Service, College of Agriculture, E. M. 3540, Washington State University, Pullman, Wash. 99163. 62¢

Soil Sanitation Procedures for the Home Gardener, Cooperative Extension Service, College of Agriculture, E. M. 3844, Washington State University, Pullman, Wash. 99163. 5¢

Sweet Corn, That Home Garden Favorite For Good Nutrition and Eating Pleasure

by E. V. Wann

Sweet corn is a common item in most American home gardens. It provides a delightful addition to everyday meals, and in season the roasting ears are enjoyed for picnics and cookouts. Since the days of the Pilgrims, corn-on-the-cob has been a popular American favorite. Sweet corn—either fresh, frozen or canned—may be served as a separate dish or used in succotash (an American Indian dish), custards, puddings, fritters, souffles, and stuffed peppers, or added to soups and chowders. Sweet corn may also be used in relishes and mixed pickles.

Most gardeners will regard sweet corn as an essential item in their garden and take great pride in the good nutrition and eating pleasure it affords.

Corn (*Zea mays*) is a member of the grass family, which includes other cereal crops such as wheat, oats, barley, sorghum, and rice. Corn is conveniently divided into six types based on its use and kernel characteristics. These are dent corn, sweet corn, popcorn, flint corn, flour corn and pod corn. They are all of the same species but differ genetically. Dent corn, sweet corn, and popcorn are the most commonly grown for their food and feed value throughout the world.

Sweet corn is believed by most authorities to have originated in North America as a mutation from field corn. The first references to sweet corn date from 1779; an 8-rowed, red-cob type called Susquehanna, or Papoon, was introduced that year near

Plymouth, Mass. In Thomas Jefferson's *Garden Book* (1810) "shriveled corn" is mentioned, which is obviously sweet corn.

By 1828 "sugar corn" was listed in New England seed catalogs. Also, evidence indicates sweet corn was being grown by the American Indians of the upper Missouri by 1833. Another early reference to sweet corn appeared in the *Travel Letters* (1821) of Timothy Dwight as being the most delicious vegetable of any known in this country.

Sweet corn as a specific crop must have come into existence at least by 1820 and reached sufficient popularity by 1828 to be in a seed catalog. The subsequent history of sweet corn is one of variety development. By 1900 there were no less than 63 varieties, and the first F_1 hybrid was introduced about 1924. Today, there are well over 200 varieties and hybrids available to sweet corn growers and gardeners.

Sweet corn differs from the other types of corn primarily by its ability to produce and retain greater quantities of sugar in the kernels. This characteristic is conditioned by a single recessive gene called *sugary-1*, symbolized su_1. Other less pronounced differences are its tender kernels at edible maturity, refined flavors, a tendency to produce suckers at the base of the plant, and wrinkled seeds when dried. Dent corn is considered the "normal" type with all the other types being genetic variation (mutations) of it. Popcorn, for example, has very hard starch in the kernels that expands explosively when heated, thus producing the fluffy white popcorn kernel.

In recent years a new kind of sweet corn has come into use that is sweeter

E. V. Wann is Research Geneticist and Laboratory Director at the U. S. Vegetable Laboratory, Agricultural Research Service, Charleston, S.C.

181

Terence O'Driscoll

than the standard sweet corn. Its sweetness is not conditioned by the *sugary-1* gene but by a similar genetic factor designated *shrunken-2* (sh_2). This gene conditions an even higher level in sugar in the kernels, giving them a sweeter taste and prolonging the edible state by three or four days.

The different types of corn should never be planted together at the same time. Pollen from dent corn or popcorn will contaminate sweet corn, causing the kernels to be starchy and not sweet. Likewise, the standard sweet varieties should not be interplanted at the same time with the extra sweet (*shrunken-2*) varieties, as the pollen from one will contaminate the other—destroying the quality of both. If both types are to be planted they should be separated by at least 400 yards distance, or one planted about four weeks after the other so

they are not pollinating at the same time.

Climatic Needs

Sweet corn is essentially a warm-weather crop. It is easily killed by frost and may be seriously injured by prolonged temperatures several degrees above freezing. Germination and emergence of the seedlings are delayed and may be prevented by soil temperatures below 50° F. Sweet corn does best in areas having mean temperatures of 65° to 75° during the required 65- to 100-day growing season. In the Northeast and North Central States this corresponds to the months June, July and August. In central and south Florida, on the other hand, sweet corn is planted fall, winter and spring. Generally, sweet corn can be grown successfully in the proper season from Mexico to Canada and in many other parts of the world.

Sweet corn will grow satisfactorily on a wide range of soil types as long as they are friable and well drained. However, a deep, loamy, naturally rich soil is preferred. Soil should be only moderately acid (pH 5.8 to 6.8). If the pH is lower than 5.8, lime should be applied. Have soil tests made to determine the proper kind and amount of lime and fertilizer to apply. Consult your local Agricultural Extension Agent since most States have laboratories that provide a soil testing service.

Available plant nutrients are especially important early in plant growth. If the plants become nutrient-deficient and stunted, they never fully recover and the yield will be reduced. Commercial fertilizers are recommended for sweet corn on just about all soils throughout the country. Fertilizer recommendations for sweet corn vary for different sections of the country and from one soil type to

Well-filled ear of sweet corn.

another. Again, depend on soil testing for specific recommendations.

Some general fertilizer recommendations for typical soils follow:

• On light sandy soils of the Atlantic and Gulf Coastal Plains, broadcast 20 pounds of 10-10-10 fertilizer per 1,000 square feet of area before planting. Then apply a side dress of nitrogen when the corn is in the 6 to 8 leaf stage at the rate of about a half pound of actual nitrogen (N) per 100 feet of row (note that Ammonium Nitrate contains 33 percent actual N and Sodium Nitrate contains 16 percent).

• On soil of average fertility in the Northeast, apply 15 to 18 pounds of 5-10-5 per 1,000 square feet of area prior to planting and about 3 pounds of the same fertilizer banded per 100 feet of row at the time of planting.

• In the more fertile valleys of the West and Pacific Northwest and on the rich soils of the Midwest corn belt, apply in bands 3 to 5 pounds of 5-10-5 per 100 feet of row at the time of planting.

The broadcast applications are usually worked into the soil before planting. The band applications should be made when the seedbed is prepared, about 3 inches to the sides of the row of seed and 1 to 2 inches deeper than the seed is planted. The above rates are based on rows spaced 3 feet apart.

Moisture Needs

Sweet corn requires a continuous and adequate moisture supply for satisfactory growth and yield. In non-irrigated areas of the United States, sweet corn is grown with reasonable success where the rainfall from April through September is 20 inches or more and fairly well distributed. Unless the soil can retain a large supply of water, sweet corn will suffer from lack of moisture if rainless periods last more than 2 weeks during the growing season.

In the South and Southwest, after the tassels show, the plants need rain or irrigation every week. For these areas, and where soil moisture is likely to be depleted, it is advisable to provide some supplemental irrigation. Furrow irrigation is satisfactory in most soils where runoff can be controlled.

Sweet corn varieties differ in the way their growth is affected by day length. Early maturing varieties developed for the North are not recommended for the South. They are adapted to the long, cool summer days in the North and do not make satisfactory growth in the deep South. Conversely the southern varieties are not adapted to the North. When planted in the North they may not silk and tassel until they reach 8 to 12 feet in height, and it is too late for them to produce edible corn before frost. Therefore, specific varieties are recommended for different sections of the country.

Hybrids

F_1 hybrids have largely replaced the open-pollinated varieties. As with all hybrid plants, new seed must be obtained for each crop. Seed saved from the hybrid plants will not reproduce true to type and will not retain the hybrid vigor of the parent plants. Several public research agencies and private companies breed and introduce new varieties of sweet corn. As a result, a large number of excellent hybrids are available for gardeners. Some hybrids will be available for only a few years, being replaced by better ones.

Sweet corn variety trials are conducted each year by many State agricultural experiment stations, and lists of recommended varieties are published based on these trials. Contact your State agricultural extension service for a list of varieties recommended specifically for your area.

Sweet corn requires plenty of space

and is adapted only to larger gardens exposed to full sunlight. It does best planted in rows 30 to 36 inches apart with single plants spaced 12 to 16 inches apart in the row. Overcrowding the corn will reduce the ear yield drastically. Planting four or more short rows is better than one long row to insure complete pollination. If the prevailing wind is across the row, pollen will be carried away from the silks and result in poorly filled ears.

To conserve space in the garden, corn may be planted next to vine crops, such as cucumber and cantaloupe. As the vines grow, they will grow between the corn plants.

Proper seedbed preparation is important for sweet corn in the garden since herbicides are generally not used. A clean freshly worked seedbed enables the seedling to emerge rapidly and get off to a good start ahead of grass and weeds. Seed should be planted to a depth of about 1 inch in moist, heavy soils and 1 to 2 inches in light, sandy soils, depending on the moisture conditions at planting time.

It is generally a good idea to plant at approximately twice the desired stand and thin to single stalks at the desired spacing after the seedlings have become well established. This will allow for any reduction in seed germination and for loss of a few emerging seedlings to insects, birds and other garden pests. About a quarter pound of seed is sufficient for each 100 feet of row.

Successive plantings are recommended in order to provide a steady supply of fresh corn throughout the practical harvest season. Also, an early, followed by a full season variety, may be planted at the same time to give a prolonged harvest period.

Once the desired stand has been established, the area should be kept free of weeds by cultivation and hoeing.

Diseases: Diseases are generally not a serious threat to clean, well nourished sweet corn plantings. Those that do occur most frequently are seedling root rot, Stewart's bacterial wilt, and common corn smut.

Root rot is caused by rot-producing fungi in the soil. It is often associated with a damp, cold soil, and may be evident as a slight stunting and irregular plant growth. Seed treatment with a fungicide provides good protection for the seedling during its early growth. Most sweet corn seeds packaged and sold commercially today have been treated with a fungicide. Use treated seeds whenever practical.

Stewart's wilt may appear at any stage of growth, but is most noticeable when plants attain considerable size. It produces yellow to brown streaks up to an inch wide on the leaves, and may extend the entire length of the leaf. Brown discoloration and sunken cavities form in the stalk near the soil line. Plants that become infected early may wilt and die. Those infected later may be only stunted and have streaked leaves.

The disease tends to be more prevalent after mild winters and is known to be spread by corn flea beetle. There are no sprays or seed treatments effective for controlling this disease.

Where wilt is suspected of becoming a problem, resistant varieties should be planted. Most varieties developed in recent years are resistant to the disease, particularly among the full season maturity group.

Common smut is characterized by the presence of large, fleshy galls on the stalks, leaves, tassel and ears. At first the galls are silvery white and spongy. Later, they turn brown or black, rupture and release large masses of powdery black spores. Smut galls are unsightly and render the affected ears inedible. Smut is promoted by injuries to the plant during cultivation, by insects, or hail.

Again, there are no chemical treatments to control the disease.

The best means of control is to avoid injuring the plants, avoid areas where smut occurred the previous year, and remove and destroy smut galls before they break open. This last step will prevent the spores from being released to infect later plantings.

Corn earworm.

Insects: Many species of insects are known to attack and damage sweet corn at all stages of its growth. Those that attack the plants early are more apt to cause serious damage, and they need to be dealt with promptly. These include the southern corn rootworm, cutworms, white grubs, wireworms and flea beetles. You can get some protection against the rootworms, wireworms, and grubs by using seed treated with a combination fungicide-insecticide. Cutworms and flea beetles may require an application of insecticide for control.

Insects attacking sweet corn later in its growth are corn borers, armyworms, aphids and the corn earworm.

Several insecticides are available to control them. Recommendations for specific compounds to use and rates of application can usually be obtained from a reputable garden supply center.

Once the sweet corn becomes established and attains most of its plant growth it can withstand a surprising amount of insect feeding without drastic loss of yield. Earworms that begin feeding on the silks and burrow into the ear tips are difficult to control. Unless the infestation is extremely high and damaging, most gardeners choose to ignore the worm at the tip of the ear, merely clipping off the ear tip and any damaged kernels when the corn is husked.

Most State agricultural experiment stations publish current recommendations for controlling insects on sweet corn. These bulletins and circulars can be obtained by writing to your State Agricultural Extension Service.

Harvesting

Sweet corn should be harvested when the kernels are in the milk stage. At this stage the silks are brown and dry beyond the end of the husks and the ear has enlarged enough to fill the husks tightly to the tip. The kernels are about as large as they will become, but they are still soft, tender and filled with an opaque milky juice.

With some experience the optimum maturity for harvest can be recognized by sight and feel. The husks should never be disturbed to peek at the corn as this will permit insects and birds to invade the ear.

Another way to estimate harvest time is to note the date of silk emergence on the earliest plants in a row, then harvest those ears 17 to 24 days later. The number of days from silk emergence to prime harvest will vary according to weather conditions. If days and nights are exceptionally

the plant. For best quality, the corn should be picked early in the morning and refrigerated immediately. The sooner it is prepared for serving the better, but it can be held in a refrigerator (35 to 40° F) for 2 to 3 days with only a moderate reduction in eating quality.

To harvest corn, break the ear shank as close to the ear as practicable without breaking the main stalk or tearing the entire shank from the stalk. Grasp the ear with one hand near its base and bend it sharply downward or to one side with a rotary motion of the wrist. The inexperienced may need to use both hands; hold the shank with one hand and use the other to snap the ear off. With practice and a strong grip, the ears of most varieties can be snapped off with one hand.

Many of the modern hybrids under optimum fertility and growing conditions will produce two nice ears per plant. The top ear will be the dominant one, and it will reach prime maturity a day or so ahead of the second ear. Under such conditions a 100-foot row should yield 100 to 120 nice ears.

warm, prime maturity may be reached 17 or 18 days after silking. If cooler weather prevails during this period, it may require 22 to 24 days. After picking a few ears, you usually can make an accurate determination about harvesting the remainder of the corn at its prime maturity.

Sweet corn passes through its prime maturity very quickly. With uniform hybrid varieties the harvest of a single planting will last only about 4 to 5 days. If harvest is delayed the kernels become tough, starchy and lose their sweet flavor.

Sweet corn also loses its quality rapidly after it has been picked from

Fully mature and well-developed ears of sweet corn.

Cucurbit Crops—Cucumbers, Gourds, Melons, Pumpkins, Squash—Have Uniform Needs

by *Thomas W. Whitaker*

Cucurbit crops should be staples for home gardeners from Maine to California. Cucumbers, gourds, muskmelons, pumpkins, squash, and watermelons will perform satisfactorily over a wide range of climate and soil conditions. The vine, or more properly, the cucurbit crops are extremely uniform in their environmental and cultural requirements. Thus, a set of procedures designed for the culture of cucumbers can be used equally well for raising squash, with perhaps some slight modification.

The wide adaptation of the cucurbit crops to culture in temperate zone areas is surprising because they are basically tropical or semi-tropical plants, annuals, extremely frost tender, and mostly incapable of functioning normally at temperatures below 60° F. For best seed germination, temperatures of 60° to 75° are required, and for maximum seasonal growth, average mean temperatures of 65° to 85° are needed.

Considering their tropical origins, the cucurbits should thrive during the long, hot, humid days and warm nights of summer in the north temperate zone—and they do. Under such circumstances, and with adequate soil moisture from rainfall or irrigation, the vines grow rapidly and respond by quickly producing fruit. Summer squash and pickling cucumbers will produce an edible product within 48 to 56 days from planting. Muskmelons require 130 to 140 days from planting. Some baking squash, pumpkins and gourds have best quality if the harvest is delayed until after the

vines are senescent or have been killed by frost.

The cucurbit crops are a homogenous group, easily identified by their prostrate, sprawling vines, usually with tendrils. Each runner bears many large, lobed more or less palmate leaves (having the shape of a palm leaf). Except for the bottle gourd, the flowers are usually bright yellow, large and conspicuous. The bottle gourd has white flowers which open at night. They are pollinated by noctural insects.

Each vine bears two kinds of flowers; the large or pistillate (no anthers, female), and the smaller or staminate (no pistils, male). Commercial varieties of muskmelons have a variation on the basic pattern. In this group, perfect flowers (with both pistillate and staminate parts) are on the same plant with staminate flowers.

The botanical name for the fruit of a cucurbit is a pepo. A pepo is a fleshy, indehiscent (closed at maturity), berry-like structure, the product of an inferior ovary. Some of the fruits of cucurbits are among the largest in the plant kingdom. Squashes weighing 350 pounds have been reliably reported, and fruits of the bottle gourd are nearly as large.

The most obvious disadvantages of cucurbit crops from the viewpoint of the home gardener are their light and space requirements. They need maximum sunshine for best development. A few vigorous plants of pumpkin, watermelon or gourd can overwhelm the small garden. These disadvantages can be successfully overcome by careful site selection within the garden, by planting bush or dwarf varieties of squash, and by judicious use of a trellis, or using structures adjacent to the garden—

Thomas W. Whitaker is a Plant Geneticist (Collaborator) with the Agricultural Research Service, La Jolla, Calif.

Darrow M. Watt

Darrow M. Watt

*Top, pumpkins and winter squash —
banana, acorn, Hubbard, and butternut.
Right, youngster displays cucumber
grown in Children's Garden of Brooklyn
Botanic Garden, New York. Above, easy
does it! A little effort is worth the pies
these pumpkins will make.*

William E. Carnahan

such as fences, garages, doghouses, etc.—as a substitute for a trellis.

Nutrients. Cucurbits are not consumed primarily for their nutritional value. They contain only a sprinkling of vitamins, minerals and protein, and except for baking squashes are low in calories. Since they are low in caloric content, they are frequently used in reducing diets.

The attraction of cucurbit fruits as food is mostly to the palate. Their aroma, flavor, texture, and juiciness are among the most attractive and delightful in the vegetable world. Muskmelons make a superb breakfast fruit or dessert; besides they are relatively high in vitamins A and C. The cool, crisp, juicy, refreshing taste of a watermelon on a warm summer day is an unforgettable experience. Cucumbers, fresh or pickled, are zesty ingredients of salads and sandwiches. Summer squash, boiled and seasoned, is an extremely tasty dish, and baked squash is comparable to sweet potatoes as a dietary staple. The dessert qualities of pumpkin pie are well-known.

Cucurbits are raised mostly for their fruits which are consumed in the immature stage (summer squash, pickles), or mature stage (muskmelons, watermelons, winter squash). Gourds are allowed to mature, and then can be used as ornamentals, planters, liquid containers, work baskets, rattles, drums, etc. As food, the cucurbits can be boiled, baked, stewed, dried, pickled, or eaten uncooked. In Latin America, the staminate flowers of squash are dipped in a batter, fried, and served as a fritter. Watermelon rinds are delicious pickled or candied.

There are reasons for thinking that squashes and pumpkins were originally domesticated for their tasty, nutritious seeds, rather than the fruit flesh. In Mexico, squash seeds, fried in oil and salted, are sold by street venders, much like peanuts are sold at baseball games in this country. Also, in Mexico, squashes have been selected for the number and quality of their seeds as food, while the flesh is ignored.

Soils. The cucurbits are not exacting in their soil requirements. They accept almost any good garden soil, well-drained, aerated, and enriched with a generous supply of plant compost or animal manures. Sandy loams which warm up quickly in the spring are preferred for an early maturing crop, but crops can be grown on heavier soils if they are properly managed. Heavier soils have greater water-holding capacity, hence they withstand droughty conditions much better than lighter soils.

One factor that places a definite limit on the culture of cucurbit crops is soil pH. They are uniformly sensitive to acidic soils, and they require a neutral (pH 7) or even better soil with a slightly alkaline reaction. For acidic soils, treatment with lime prior to planting is mandatory.

Nutrient Needs

While cucurbit crops do moderately well on most fertile soils, they benefit greatly from a generous supply of organic material in the form of green and animal manures. Well-composted animal manures worked into the soil and concentrated in the area where the seed is expected to be planted (hills) is the most efficient means of using these materials. In addition to manures, applying mineral fertilizers is usually needed for a satisfactory crop. Fertilizers act as a supplement to the manure and provide an added source of plant nutrients during the growing season.

It is difficult to be specific about fertilizer recommendations because of great variation in soil types, soil fertility, and other soil conditions. In general, cucurbit crops can be expected to respond to a complete fertilizer containing 4 to 6 pct nitrogen,

Spacing Distances, Planting Depths for Cucurbit Crops
Measurements are in Inches

Crop	Spacing Between plants in row	Spacing Between rows	Planting Depth
Cucumber	12 [1] 24–36 [2]	48–72	1
Muskmelon	12 [1] 24–36 [2]	60–84	1–1½
Pumpkin	36–40	72–96	2–3
Squash (bush)	24–30	36	2–3
Squash (vining)	36–40	72–96	2–3
Gourd	36–40	72–96	2–3
Watermelon	24–36 [1] 72 [2]	72–84	1–2

[1] Single plants.
[2] Hills.

8 to 10 pct phosphoric acid, and 5 to 10 pct potash. This translates into 1 to 2 tablespoons for each hill prior to planting. In light, sandy soils, that leach readily, one or two side dressings of ammonium sulphate may be needed during the season; perhaps a tablespoon per hill will suffice.

In the garden, cucurbit crops are normally planted in hills, specific spacing depending upon the crop. In commercial practice, however, cucumbers, muskmelons, bush squash, and watermelons are drilled in continuous rows, and thinned to stand.

Cucurbit seeds are relatively large, and should be covered to a depth of 1 to 3 inches. After covering, the soil is lightly tamped, but not so firmly as to create a crust. In light, sandy soils that tend to dry out rapidly, seeds should be planted at greater depth than in heavier soils.

Assuming normal germination (80 to 90 pct), 4 to 5 seeds are planted in each hill. Thin the seedlings when they have 2 to 3 leaves. Remove all but 1 or 2 large, healthy, well-spaced plants per hill. More than 2 plants per hill causes undesirable crowding, and competition for nutrients, water and light. Under such conditions, the final result is unthrifty plants and declining yields.

Irrigation. In the West and Southwest, cucurbit crops are totally dependent upon irrigation as a source of moisture, and even in the Midwest and East some form of supplementary irrigation may be desirable during drought periods. The cucurbits are moderately deep-rooted crops, filling the soil mass to a depth of three feet or more. This means the soil must be supplied with enough moisture to maintain a thoroughly moist condition to this depth.

Furrow irrigation is probably the most practical for home gardens, especially after the young plants have a dozen or more true leaves. Moisture on the leaves from whatever source encourages several foliar diseases difficult to suppress with fungicides. Hence, sprinkler irrigation is not recommended if alternative methods are available.

Mulching and weed control are not critical for growing cucurbits in the home garden. If the soil directly above the seed (the hills) is kept from crusting, no mulch is needed. A thick, hard crust will prevent emergence of the young seedlings. Therefore, after planting and firming, it is important to scatter a thin layer of loose soil over seed in the hill.

There is really no safe, effective chemical weed control for cucurbit crops. If planting is done in a well-prepared seed bed, weeds will seldom be a problem and can easily be controlled by hand or by hoe. The cucurbits are leafy, rapidly growing, vigorous plants. Consequently, as they grow older they tend to shade out competition from weeds. Usually weeds are not much of a problem until late in the season, but by this time the crop is mature and little harm will be done.

The cucurbits are subject to infection by several diseases and attack by insects that can damage or even destroy a potentially promising crop without much warning, and within a relatively short time period. Nearly all the important pests are destructive to cucurbits you are likely to plant in the home garden. There are exceptions, however, such as scab, a fungus damaging only to cucumbers, and anthracnose, also a fungus, commonly attacking only watermelon. Squash bug and squash vine borer are more of a problem on squashes and pumpkins than with other cucurbits.

Cucumber Beetles

Bacteria responsible for bacterial wilt are spread by cucumber beetles. This fact is the key to control. If the beetles are eliminated or reduced to low levels in the garden, bacterial wilt will not be a problem. The bacteria multiply rapidly and plug the water transportation system of the plant. This results in characteristic wilting of the vegetative parts. Older plants at first may have only one shoot affected, but later the entire plant will wilt and die. Younger plants die quickly. It helps to promptly remove infected plants from the garden.

Anthracnose, a disease of watermelon, flourishes in warm, moist weather, and is particularly troublesome in the Southeast. Under favorable conditions it also attacks cucumbers and muskmelons, but is an acute hazard only to watermelon production. The symptoms are small, round, water-soaked spots on the fruits. These spots later become enlarged, sunken, with dark centers, which may turn pinkish in moist, humid weather. Infected leaves have a scorched appearance, and the stems may be girdled. Vines with the disease may die. The fruits are worthless, often decaying before they are mature.

A few simple preventive measures often give satisfactory control if you are in an area where anthracnose is a problem. (a) Plant seed of varieties known to have a high level of resistance to the disease. (b) Plant seed that has been treated with a fundicide to remove spores of the fungus. (c) Practice garden sanitation, removing all the debris of cucurbit vines because the spores overwinter in this trash. (d) Select areas for planting that have not been used for cucurbit crops within the past 3 to 4 years.

Downy mildew fungus is a destructive disease of cucurbits, especially when meteorological conditions favor its rapid growth. Warm, moist conditions that occur at times during the growing season in the Atlantic and Gulf States are ideal for growth of downy mildew. However, low humidity, high temperatures and lack of free moisture on the leaves and stems immediately check the fungus growth. Spores of the fungus are produced on the underside of the leaves, and are spread by wind or splashing of raindrops.

Initial symptoms are small, yellowish spots, with irregular edges which appear on the leaves at about the time the vines commence to set fruit. Tissue at the center of each spot soon turns brown and dies. Later the spots become more numerous, coalesce, and the leaf shrivels and dies. The brown or blackish withered leaves curl upward, a characteristic that makes downy mildew easy to identify with certainty. The fruits are not attacked, but fruits from denuded vines are apt to lack flavor, be tasteless, and are practically inedible.

Whenever possible use varieties with some tolerance or even resistance to the disease. Generally the home gardener will have to lean heavily on the use of a suitable fungicide.

Powdery mildew fungus can be a devastating pest of nearly all cucurbits, except watermelons. The first symptoms are small, white patches on undersides of the older leaves. As the disease increases in intensity, leaves and stems become covered with the white, powdery spore masses. The foliage gradually dies, leaving the fruit exposed to the sun. In muskmelons, such fruits ripen prematurely, and are usually sunburned and of poor quality.

The fungus responsible for powdery mildew requires much sunshine and reasonably high temperatures for best growth. Rains and low light intensity tend to check its rampant increase.

Resistant Varieties

Resistant or tolerant varieties of most species are available, and should be used where powdery mildew is likely to be a problem. Several safe chemicals are effective against powdery mildew.

Scab is caused by a fungus which attacks the fruit, particularly cucumber, but it may occasionally damage young squash fruits. Sunken, dark brown, irregular spots appear on the fruits from which a gummy substance is extruded. The young fruits become malformed and cannot be used.

The disease spreads rapidly in cool, moist weather. It is most serious on cucumbers in the northern tier of States (Wisconsin, Michigan, Minnesota, New York and Maine). Good garden sanitation and use of resistant varieties should successfully solve this problem for the home gardener.

Mosaic caused by virus is one of the most widespread and serious diseases of cucurbits. Characteristic symptoms are light-green mottling of the leaves, and the younger leaves are malformed, dwarfed, and slightly curled. With late infection, the symptoms are mild and little harm is done to the crop. Vines infected in early stages of development normally are dwarfed, the leaves and flowers malformed, and they do not produce acceptable fruit.

There are roughly two classses of virus that attack cucurbits. (1) Watermelon mosaic viruses which are not seed-borne, and are spread by sucking insects—chiefly aphids. (2) Squash mosaic viruses, which are seed-borne and are spread by chewing insects—chiefly cucumber beetles.

The watermelon mosaic viruses are destructive pests of cucurbits because they are spread by aphids, and it is almost impossible to deny aphids access to home gardens. Apparently the virus is carried by several widely grown ornamentals, so sources of the virus are always present. Control is difficult, although there are resistant or tolerant varieties of cucumber, but resistance breeding programs in other species are not well-developed.

Control of the squash mosaic viruses can be established by planting virus-free seed. Also, controlling cucumber beetles and other chewing insects prevents dissemination of the virus.

Root knot disease is caused by minute eelworms or nematodes which enter the roots where they feed and breed. Feeding causes the root tissues to swell, producing nodules or galls on the roots. Some galls are small, others may be the size of a walnut. Plants become dwarfed, unthrifty, and often turn yellow and die. Soil heavily infested with nematodes should be fumigated, using one of the several nematocides that are effective when properly applied. Fumigation will reduce the population of nematodes to a point where good crops can be grown for at least 1 to 2 years. Some control can be obtained by crop rotation, that is, by not planting susceptible crops in the same soil for 3 to 5 years. Much research has been done, but resistant varieties are not yet available.

Cucumber beetles, both striped and 12-spotted, are common pests in most gardens. It is important to control them because the adults seriously damage or totally destroy the plants, and their activities also spread certain diseases of cucurbits (bacterial wilt, squash mosaic). Additionally, the larvae bore into roots and stems below the soil line, often causing the plants to suddenly wilt and die. There are satisfactory chemicals that will control these insects, but they must be applied at the first appearance of the beetles for acceptable control.

Aphids—small, fragile, soft-bodied insects with sucking mouth parts—can be a problem on cucurbits during the course of the growing season. Aphids come in several colors, such

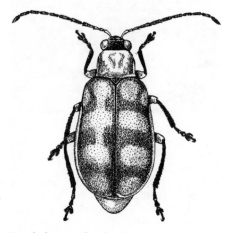

Banded cucumber beetle.

as black, green, yellow, or pink. They feed on the undersides of leaves, causing a curling or cupping. With severe infection, the leaves become sticky, lose color, and the plant dies. Winged females fly from plant to plant, establishing new colonies. Aphids can be controlled by chemicals, but be sure to use those insecticides that are least harmful to aphid predators.

The squash bug is a troublesome pest of squash and pumpkins, and occasionally attacks gourds. Adults and the immature forms (nymphs) suck the sap from leaves and stems,

causing the plant to wilt and die. The adult bug is about a half inch long, and dirty brownish, or black. The nymphs are much smaller and steel-grey. The female deposits the relatively large and brownish eggs in regularly arranged masses on the underside of the leaves.

Good plant sanitation helps control this pest. Promptly remove and destroy debris from cucurbit vines and fruit. You can trap the bugs by placing a shingle or board at the base of the plants. The bugs collect here during the night, and can be destroyed the following morning before they become active. Also, searching out the egg masses and destroying them can be helpful. Insecticides are effective against heavy infestations.

The squash vine borer can damage squash and pumpkin in areas east of the Rocky Mountains. The borer is the larval stage of a day-flying moth that deposits her eggs on the stem of the plant, slightly above the soil line. The young borers penetrate the stem and burrow toward the base. When mature, the borer crawls from the plant to the soil where it pupates.

Garden sanitation, and fall tillage deep enough to destroy the cocoons, are effective control measures. Also, where only a few plants are involved, locate the wound and slit the stem with a razor blade or sharp knife, thus puncturing the borer. Then place moist soil around the stem to a height a little beyond the wound. New roots will develop, thus compensating for the injury.

Harvesting. The proper time to harvest is crucial for obtaining maximum quality of cucurbit fruits. Cucumbers for pickling should be harvested when the young fruits attain a length of 2 to 4 inches, roughly 3 to 4 days after the flower has opened. For dill and larger pickles, harvest is delayed until fruits are 6 inches or more in length. The slicing type is harvested when the fruit is 8 to 10 inches long.

For muskmelons, nature has provided an unmistakeable sign. At maturity, an abscission layer forms between stem and fruit. This layer appears as a crack, completely encircling the stem, at the point of attachment to the fruit. If the stem has to be forcibly separated from the fruit, the fruit is immature. The abscission layer, or "slip" as it is known in the trade, is characteristic of most muskmelon varieties except the casabas and honeydews. Maturity in the latter is judged by softening of the blossom end of the fruit, and subtle changes in the fruit's color.

The expertise required to select a watermelon at prime maturity is only acquired by experience. For the amateur, some of the guesswork can be eliminated by rapping the melon sharply with the knuckles. A crisp, metallic sound indicates immaturity, while a dull, flat sound suggests maturity. Also, at maturity the ground spot usually changes from white to light yellow.

Summer squash, which is consumed in the immature state, is best harvested when 3 to 6 inches long, about 3 to 4 days after the pistillate flower opens. At this stage summer squash is tender, crisp, and has a good flavor. It should be harvested 2 to 3 times per week.

Winter squash, or baking squash, normally is harvested when mature. Maturity can be roughly estimated by pressure from the thumbnail on the fruit exterior. If the skin is hard and impervious to scratching, the fruit is mature.

Fruits of pumpkins and gourds are customarily allowed to remain in the garden until frost destroys the vines, or they deteriorate.

Storage. Most cucurbit fruits are consumed fresh. Honeydew and casaba muskmelons can be stored as long as a month in a cool, dry environment. Pumpkins and the hard-shelled squashes can be stored for several months if properly cured. This means the fruit should be mature and carefully handled at harvest. After harvest, they should be placed in a room or other area with temperatures of 80° to 85° F for 10 days, then transferred to a cool, dry place, preferably with temperatures of 50° to 60°. In storage, the fruit must be well-ventilated, not piled on each other.

Since the cucurbits are large, vigorous plants, requiring relatively huge amounts of space for maximum development, the number of plants that can be accommodated in the averge garden is minimal.

Plant population should be enough to cover the needs of an average family. Six cucumber plants, if harvested regularly, will produce sufficient fruit for a family. Muskmelons produce 2 to 3 fruits per plant and needs should be based on this estimate.

Watermelons are not heavy producers. Most varieties produce 1 to 2 melons per vine. Some of the varieties with small fruits are more prolific.

Two to three well-grown plants of bush summer squash will produce an abundance of squash for the average family and the neighbors, if harvested at regular intervals. For the average garden, 4 to 6 vine type squash or pumpkin should be sufficient.

Gourds are terrifically prolific. Two or three vines on a trellis will produce 12 to 24 fruits depending upon the variety.

Thump test tells this young feller his icebox watermelon is ripe. But the most definite proof (and the most fun) comes from taste-test.

Photos by William Aplin

195

Asparagus Starts Up Slow But Goes On and On; Rhubarb Also Takes Its Own Sweet Time

ASPARAGUS

by Stephen A. Garrison and
J. Howard Ellison

The cultivated asparagus plant, Asparagus officinalis, is a perennial vegetable that can thrive in the home garden for 25 years or more when well cared for. However, plants may have to grow 3 years before they can be harvested.

The underground root system consists of an extensive network of fleshy storage roots with small feeder roots that absorb water and nutrients. The storage roots are about the diameter of a pencil and may be 5 to 10 feet long in mature plants, depending on the soil type in which the plants are growing.

These storage roots are attached to an underground stem called a rhizome. The storage roots and the rhizome are commonly referred to as an asparagus crown. When the soil is warm and the soil moisture favorable, buds arise from the rhizome and develop into edible spears, utilizing the carbohydrate and other nutrient reserves present in the storage roots.

The spears which are not harvested develop into attractive, green, fern-like stalks (brush). Through photosynthesis, the mature plant produces carbohydrates and synthesizes other essential nutrients that are translocated to the storage roots. The stored reserves supply the energy required to produce spears during the following growing season.

For this reason it is important to protect the fern-like foliage from in-sects, diseases, and other injury before natural senescence and cold weather terminate the functioning of the green foliage in the fall.

Spears should not be removed from the plants during the first two growing seasons in the permanent location. (See harvesting details later in chapter).

Unlike most plants that have both male and female parts on the same plant, the asparagus plant is dioecious. The male flowers that produce pollen are present on one plant and the female flowers that produce the berries and the seeds are on a separate plant. Bees transfer the pollen from the male to the female flowers.

Research has shown that female plants, which expend much energy in producing fruits and seeds, do not yield as well and are not as long-lived as male plants.

The genus Asparagus, a member of the Lily family, originated along the shores of the Mediterranean Sea and on its many islands. Asparagus (Asparagus officinalis) was considered a delicacy by the ancient Greeks. The elder Cato discussed its cultivation in 200 B.C., and 200 years later Pliny described the spear size of asparagus. A. W. Kidner, writing in England in 1959, said the spear size described by Pliny was very similar to that in England more than 19 centuries later. It is remarkable how little the cultivated asparagus has changed since the time of Christ.

Most asparagus strains grown in the United States today are seedling populations selected from the Martha and Mary Washington strains developed in the early 1900's by J. B. Norton of the U.S. Department of Agriculture.

All presently available asparagus strains produce plants with variable vigor, size and disease resistance.

Stephen A. Garrison and J. Howard Ellison are Associate Professor and Professor respectively in Vegetable Crops, Rutgers University, New Brunswick, N.J.

Terence O Driscoll

Emerging asparagus spear.

Plant breeders are developing more uniform plants by reproducing highly selected parent clones through test-tube tissue culture. In the near future, gardeners will be able to purchase these high-yielding uniform seeds or even highly selected, extremely productive clones propagated by tissue culture.

The Viking strain is suggested for gardeners in the northern United States. For the West Coast, California U.C. 157 is recommended. In the East and Midwest, Rutgers Beacon, Waltham Washington, and local selections of the "Washington" type are recommended to home gardeners and are available through the major seed distributors.

Asparagus is low in calories, but high in flavor. A serving of 4 spears of asparagus (60 grams) contains just 10 calories, 1 gram of protein, 2 grams of carbohydrates, and only traces of fat. When the nutrient content of vegetables is compared, asparagus is a good source of vitamin A and riboflavin, and a very good source of thiamin.

Environment Needs

Able to tolerate great variations in temperature, asparagus grows in places such as the Imperial Valley of southern California, where the temperature soars to 115° to 120° F in the summer, or Minnesota, where winter minimums of 40° below zero occur.

However, asparagus grows best where the growing season is long and the days are sunny for maximum photosynthesis. Ideal day temperatures during the growing season are 75° to 85° F, and nighttime readings in the 60's to minimize respiration. These conditions favor maximum storage of carbohydrates in the root system for high yield and quality of spears the following season.

Asparagus can be a home garden vegetable in most parts of the country except the Deep South. Asparagus does not grow well in the Gulf Coast States, due to the moist, warm winters which may stimulate sporadic growth during winter.

Asparagus can be grown on a wide range of soil textures from loamy sands to clay loams as long as water drainage and aeration are good. In the more arid regions the heavy soils are satisfactorily aerated and produce excellent asparagus. However, in regions of moderate to high rainfall, asparagus grows best on deep, well-drained sandy loam soils. Asparagus plants lose vigor, become more susceptible to root rot, and die in poorly drained areas or following prolonged high rainfall.

The soil reaction (pH) should be maintained between 6.5 and 6.8. Medium fertility is best, to provide a balance between top growth and root growth, but the plant has a relatively high potassium requirement for maximum production.

Growing

In the past, most garden asparagus has been started by planting crowns.

Plant only healthy 1-year-old crowns and never use 2- or 3-year-old crowns. It is difficult to obtain commercial crowns free of Fusarium root rot (see discussion later in chapter). Fusarium carried on the seed will infect young seedlings and contaminate the garden permanently.

One way to avoid Fusarium is to plant asparagus seed that has been surface-sterilized. You can use this seed to grow your own crowns or seedling transplants.

Crowns are produced by seeding a nursery about 2 weeks before tomatoes are normally transplanted into the garden. Seed is sown 1 inch deep and 3 inches apart in the row with 2½ feet between rows in the nursery. Plant 3 to 4 seeds for each crown you want to plant in the permanent bed. The following spring (February-March), when the plants are still dormant and the ground has thawed, carefully dig the crowns to minimize damage to the root system. Immediately plant the crowns in the permanent bed as described later.

To grow transplants, sow the seed 12 to 14 weeks before transplanting seedlings to the garden in the spring. The sowing date will vary from late December in the Southwest to mid-February in Northern areas of the country. Use a commercial potting mixture of peat moss and vermiculite, (pH 5.5 to 6.0) and sow two seeds ¾ inch deep in small (2-inch diameter) pots, or seed in rows in flats. The rows should be 2 inches apart with seeds 2 inches apart in the row.

Maintain the temperature at 75° to 85° F while seeds are germinating. As seedlings emerge, they should grow at 70° to 75° during the day and 65° at night. Grow the plants in a greenhouse or window with full sunlight. Use supplementary fluorescent lights to extend the day length to 12 to 14 hours when plants are not grown in the greenhouse.

Apply a soluble complete fertilizer, such as 15-15-15, at half the recommended rate 4, 8, and 12 weeks after sowing the seed. Rinse the foliage lightly with water after fertilizing to avoid fertilizer injury to the tender growth. Excessive fertilization promotes large tender tops and small root systems with limited reserves in the storage roots. Make the last application just before transplanting to the garden, after danger of the last killing frost is past. If you don't have a suitable place to grow your own seedling transplants, you may be able to get seedlings from a commercial plant grower who specializes in bedding plants.

Asparagus should be planted with other perennial crops for convenience of tillage and management. It is preferable to plant on the north or east side of the garden so as not to shade other vegetables or low-growing fruits.

Asparagus can be planted along a fence, as long as there is plenty of sun. In fact, the beautiful green, fern-like foliage grows five to six feet high, and can be used as an ornamental summer screen. The female plants produce berries that become bright red in late summer and fall. The tops turn from green to an attractive yellow in fall and brown during winter.

Before planting, broadcast and turn under 1.2 pounds of 5-10-10 fertilizer (or equivalent) per 100 square feet of area. If lime is needed, turn it under along with the fertilizer. Keep a close check on soil pH, because asparagus does poorly at pH levels below 6.0.

Plant crowns with the buds up in the bottom of a 6-inch deep V-shaped furrow, and cover with 1 to 2 inches of soil. Plant seedlings 1 inch deep on small mounds in the bottom of a similar furrow. The seedlings will require some protection from water which may stand in the furrow and from soil which can wash into the furrow. Spacing for crowns and transplants is 12 inches apart within the row and

4 to 5 feet between rows. If only one asparagus row is planted, allow at least 3 feet between the asparagus and the closest other vegetable crop.

As the asparagus grows, carefully fill in the furrow with soil so as to avoid covering any asparagus foliage. The furrows should be filled in by the end of the first growing season. Sidedress the plants with 1.2 pounds of 5-10-10 fertilizer (or equivalent) per 20 feet of row in late July or early August. Spread the fertilizer on either side of the asparagus and cultivate it lightly into the soil.

Adequate soil moisture is important during the first growing season. Don't let the plants suffer for lack of water during dry weather. Weekly applications of irrigation sufficient to wet the soil 8 inches deep should be adequate.

After the first growing season, asparagus plants do not require frequent irrigation because of the deep and extensive root system. Thorough watering (2 inches of water) slowly applied every 2 weeks during dry weather is sufficient.

During early spring of the year after planting remove the brush (old stalks) and any over-wintering weeds. Broadcast lime as needed to maintain the proper soil pH plus 1.2 pounds of 5-10-10 per 100 square feet of bed. Sidedress another 1.2 pounds of 5-10-10 per 100 square feet in late July or early August.

Remove brush during each succeeding spring before the asparagus emerges, and broadcast lime if needed. At the same time spread 3.4 pounds of 5-10-10 (or equivalent) fertilizer per 100 square feet of bed. Rake the fertilizer and lime 1 to 2 inches into the soil, taking care to avoid damage to the asparagus crowns.

Maintain good foliage growth for maximum photosynthesis. Tall weeds can shade asparagus and reduce photosynthesis. Even low weeds and grasses compete with the asparagus for water and nutrients. Thus, weed control is an important aspect of good asparagus culture. Chemical herbicides are toxic to many other vegetables and not recommended for the home garden.

Asparagus can be mulched with organic debris (leaves, grass clippings, etc.), but mulches can harbor pests, alter the soil pH, and change the crop's fertilizer needs. Clean cultivation of the asparagus is preferred.

Pests

The most serious disease of asparagus is Fusarium root rot, caused by the fungus *Fusarium oxysporum f. asparagi*. This organism is present at very low populations in most soils, where it grows slowly on organic matter in the soil.

Planting disease-free seeds or crowns of the host asparagus causes a slow build-up of the Fusarium population in the soil. However, planting infested seed or infected crowns leads to a rapid build-up that may adversely affect performance of the first asparagus planting, and permanently contaminate the garden in that location for asparagus in the future. The Fusarium infects the root system and kills the feeder roots. As a result, plant vigor declines, spear size decreases, and the weaker plants may die.

Fusarium can be identified by reddish-brown color of the feeder roots, reddish-brown spots and streaks on the storage roots, and large lesions on the base of the spears and stalks at or below the soil line.

The symptoms are much more severe when the plants are under stress due to excessively long harvests, poor drainage, competition from weeds, and damage from insects and diseases.

The best way to avoid Fusarium root rot in the garden is to plant surfaced-sterilized seed in disease-free soil. Although surface-sterilized seed is not generally available, you can treat the seed yourself.

Soak the seed for 2 minutes in a solution of 1 part laundry bleach (composed of approximately 5 percent sodium hypochlorite) plus 4 parts of water. Rinse the seeds for one minute with cool running water and plant in soil that has never grown asparagus previously, or start seedling transplants in a disease-free artificial soil mix.

Although research to control Fusarium by the use of fungicides is under way, no practical treatment is yet perfected. Progress is being made on development of Fusarium-resistant strains of asparagus at the New Jersey and California Agricultural Experiment Stations.

Rust (Puccinia asparagi) is another common fungus disease of asparagus in the East and Midwest, and certain valleys in California. Dew or other free water on the plant for 10 hours is enough for spore germination.

Ten days after germination, the fungus appears on the surface of stems and branches as small rust-colored spots, containing spores that cause spread of the disease. In the fall the rust colored areas produce black, over-wintering spores that can infect the plant the following year. Severe rust destroys much of the foliage, reducing reserves for the next year's crop.

Rust can be partially controlled by fungicides, and several asparagus strains selected in the East and Midwest have some rust resistance.

Several species of thrips are often a serious problem, primarily on small plants in a nursery or on transplanted seedlings in the garden. Thrips are small, white, flying insects which are very difficult to see. They suck plant juices and cause the green needles and stems on the young plants to turn dull gray-green, then brown. Insecticides can be used to control thrips.

The asparagus beetle (Crioceris species) is a serious pest every year, although the insect populations vary from season to season. Adult beetles, which look like slender lady-bird beetles, lay small black elongated eggs on end in rows on asparagus brush. The larvae (small, dark green worms) do the actual damage by eating the green epidermis from the fern.

Beetles can kill very young seedlings, and seriously damage fern growth of mature plants. They can be controlled by insecticides.

European asparagus aphids invaded the eastern United States in recent years. They are blue-green, with a metallic sheen (like aluminum) when in clusters on plants. The aphids feed on young growing shoots, and inhibit the elongation of internodes, producing a kind of rosette (bushy stunted growth). Heavy infestations of the insects can seriously decrease foliage area needed for photosynthesis.

Fortunately the European asparagus aphid has many natural enemies, and seems to be subsiding as a pest.

Harvesting: An important culture requirement of asparagus is that the crop must be grown for two full growing seasons before harvest begins. This is necessary to allow the plants to develop an adequate storage root system to produce spears during the first harvest season and beyond. Any harvesting or damage to the brush during the first two growing seasons dwarfs the plants and can reduce yield for the life of the bed.

When the first spears emerge in the spring, merely snap off spears 7 to 10 inches long, with tight heads, leaving the tough stub on the plant. The upper portion which snaps off should be "all green" and "all tender". Harvest all spears that come up during the harvest season.

A good general rule for length of harvest season for all areas except the cool central valleys of California is the 2-4-8 week sequence. Harvest

Asparagus spears harvested by snapping.

for 2 weeks the third year the plants are in the garden; 4 weeks the fourth year, and 8 weeks the fifth and following years. In the cool central valleys of California, a 4-8-12 week sequence is best.

When the harvest season is approximately half completed, 5 to 6 inches of soil may be carefully ridged over the row. This lowers the temperature around the crown and increases spear size. The ridge should be raked level right after the last harvest.

White asparagus, which has a distinctive flavor, can be produced by ridging 10 to 12 inches of soil over the row in the spring when the first spears emerge. When the tip of the spear breaks through the ridge of soil, carefully remove some soil from around the spear, and use a long knife or asparagus knife to cut the spear about 8 inches below the tip.

If the harvest from one day is not enough for a meal or if the asparagus is to be consumed later, wash the spears, place the cut ends in a shallow pan of water and immediately put them in the refrigerator. Good quality can be maintained for several days if the spears are kept at 35° to 40° F. A 40-foot long row of asparagus will yield approximately 10 to 25 pounds of spears during the average season.

RHUBARB
by Daniel Tompkins

Rhubarb, also known as pieplant, is a hardy perennial vegetable grown in many home gardens for its thick leaf stalks or petioles. It produces its crop early in spring, largely from food that has been stored in the large fleshy crowns and roots of the plant during the preceding year. It likes cool weather and grows best in the Northern States where the average summer temperatures are not much above 75° F. Rhubarb does not grow well in areas where the summers are quite warm.

Stalks can't be fully harvested until the third year of the planting.

A member of the buckwheat family, rhubarb is native to Central Asia. It was introduced into Great Britain, where it is grown extensively, in the 16th century and was probably brought to the United States from Italy late in the 18th century. It has long been grown in the Old World as a vegetable, an ornamental foliage plant, and for medicinal properties of the dried root which provides a strong purgative. Here in this country rhubarb is grown for its acid stalks which are stewed for pies and sauces, made into preserves, and sometimes used for making wine. It is also excellent baked.

Rhubarb leaves should never be eaten, since they contain levels of soluble oxalic acid that can make one quite ill or even cause death. The stalks are harmless since the oxalic acid is present in smaller amounts and mostly in an insoluble form.

Rhubarb contains vitamin C and calcium (largely insoluble). It also contains some vitamin A, iron, phosphorus, potassium and only about 60 calories per pound of stalks. It has been reported that rhubarb can pro-

---

Daniel Tompkins is a Horticulturist with the Cooperative State Research Service.

tect the teeth against acid erosion such as may be caused by excessive use of lemon juice or cola beverages. Rhubarb is one of the most acid of all vegetables; the juice has a pH of 3.1 to 3.2. The tender stalks are about 94 percent water.

For home use, rhubarb varieties or cultivars may be divided into two classes, those with red stalks and those with mainly green stalks when grown outdoors. The somewhat larger and more vigorous green stalk cultivars are Victoria, German Wine and Suttons' Seedless. These cultivars are commonly used by commercial growers for forcing where they produce stalks with a delicate pink-red color. The cultivars that produce red stalks when grown outdoors are Ruby, McDonald, Valentine, Canada Red, and Crimson Wine.

Rhubarb grows easily from seed but this is not recommended since many plants will not be like their parents.

Dividing Crowns

You usually propagate rhubarb by dividing the crowns in early spring. Dig the crowns and then split them into pieces with one large bud to each section of crown and root. Trim the pieces by removing all broken roots and shortening the long thin roots.

Crowns vary in size and number of buds produced due to cultivar, age, and growing conditions. Vigorous crowns will normally provide 5 to 10 pieces suitable for planting. Very old crowns may have only an outer fringe of buds suitable for dividing.

Protect the root pieces from excessive drying before planting.

Space the plants 2½ to 3 feet apart in rows 3½ to 4½ feet wide. Usually you plant in a furrow, placing the crown pieces at a depth so that the buds will not be more than two inches below the surface. Fill in soil around the pieces and firm well, but leave loose surface soil above and around the bud. The soil should be well fertilized and worked deeply and thoroughly before planting. Plant rhubarb as early in spring as the soil can be worked. For each person, about 3 to 4 plants should produce an ample supply. If well cared for, the new planting should last 5 to 7 years depending on cultivar and location.

A deep, rich, well-drained sandy loam soil is most desirable for production. However, rhubarb will grow well on any type soil from sand or peat to clay, provided it is well drained and has a good supply of moisture to encourage vigorous growth during hot summer months. Light sandy soils that warm up quickly provide earlier spring growth than the colder, heavier soils.

Rhubarb requires large amounts of plant food and abundant moisture during the growing season. If available, a heavy application of manure should be worked into the soil before planting to provide organic matter and nutrients for the growing plants. This should be followed by a manure mulch each fall.

Before planting, broadcast a complete fertilizer like 10-10-10 at the rate of 2 to 3 pounds per 100 square feet and thoroughly work it into the soil. In the following years a fertilizer like 10-10-10 should be broadcast or banded at the rate of 1½ pounds (sandy soil) to 2 pounds (clay soil) per 100 square feet before the new leaves begin to grow each spring. This fertilizer should be mixed 2 to 3 inches deep in the soil but not any closer than 10 inches from the plant.

After harvesting is completed, a sidedressing of ammonium nitrate (33.5 percent nitrogen) at the rate of 6 ounces per 100 square feet will stimulate summer growth and food storage in the roots.

If manure is not available, the rhubarb patch can be mulched with 1 to

3 inches of lawn clippings each year during late spring or early summer.

To promote good growth during the summer, water the plants whenever the soil begins to dry.

If the plants go dormant (leaves die) after harvest, little food is stored in the roots for the next year's crop.

Rhubarb is tolerant to soil acidity, and liming is seldom needed. It will grow well in soil as acid as pH 5.2, provided the essential nutrients of calcium, phosphorus, and magnesium are well supplied.

Weed control by hoeing and cultivation should be shallow and frequent enough to control emerging weeds. The most serious weed problems will usually occur early in spring before the newly planted root pieces start growing well.

When to Pick

Don't pick stalks during the first season or the year of planting. Food from the leaves is needed to enlarge the roots for the coming years' growth. During the second year stalks should be picked for only a short period (two weeks). Beginning with the third year the harvest period may extend as long as six weeks or until the stalks become small, indicating that food supplies in the roots are becoming depleted. Don't remove more than two-thirds of the developed stalks from the plant at any one time. Pull only the large stalks, leaving the young ones to grow.

Pick the stalks by pulling and not by cutting. Grasp the stalk near its base and pull it slightly to one side in the direction it grows. The stalks separate readily from the plant and are easily pulled. After the stalk is pulled, trim it by removing the leaf or leafblade.

If flower stalks appear, remove them at once so the plant's food will go into the roots for the next year's crop of stalks. Continued development of flower stalks will reduce rhubarb production during the following year.

Rhubarb is relatively free of insect and disease problems. But one insect that can cause problems is the rhubarb curculio. This snout beetle, common in the eastern half of the country, can puncture the stems—leaving black spots. The beetles average about a half-inch in length and are black. But they usually are so densely covered with a rusty powder that they appear reddish. Since the curculio as a rule feeds on curly dock weed, one control measure is to destroy these weeds growing near the rhubarb.

Phytophthora crown rot or foot rot is a disease that can affect rhubarb in the eastern half of the country. At the base of the stalk lesions develop rapidly to cause collapse of the whole stalk. In warm moist weather the stalks may continue to collapse until the plant is killed. There is no effective control at present.

Other diseases that may affect rhubarb are bacterial crown rot, pythium crown rot, rhizoctonia crown rot, gray mold or *Botrytis* (the most serious disease of commercial forcing operations), and ascochyta leaf spot. There also are a number of viruses that can reduce plant vigor and yields.

If you plan to propagate your own plants, identify the most vigorous 2- to 3-year-old plants with stakes during June. Leave the stakes by the plants (crown) until the following spring when the marked crowns are dug and split for planting stock. Replace plants when they start to produce fewer—and small size—stalks. Remove the old crowns and associated fleshy roots by digging, and make a new planting elsewhere in the garden.

Commercially, much of the rhubarb crop is produced by forcing during the winter months. This is a unique horticultural practice of producing an edible crop inside darkened, heated buildings. Rhubarb plants are grown in the field for 2 to 3 years during which the food materials produced in the leaves are stored in the thick fleshy roots. During winter months when the plant leaves are dead, the crown (roots) are brought from the field to the forcing structures. The large amount of food stored in fleshy roots of the crown enables it to produce many well-colored rhubarb stalks under the proper forcing conditions of darkness, water, and low even heat (50° to 55° F). After the crowns are forced they are discarded.

A crown can produce 4 to 12 pounds of stalks, depending on cultivar and crown size and vigor.

While it is a messy and time-consuming job, crowns may be forced in the home basement or cellar. About 6 to 10 good crowns should produce enough for the average family after you learn how to force rhubarb.

For Further Reading:

U. S. Department of Agriculture. *Rhubarb Production*, Leaflet 555, for sale by Superintendent of Documents, U.S. Government Printing Office, Washington, D.C. 20202. 25¢.

A Few Rows of Home Garden Potatoes Can Put Nutritious Food on Your Table

by Orrin C. Turnquist

The potato is probably the most important vegetable crop in the world today. None other is used as regularly and in such quantity in the average American home. Its culture is simple and it is a dependable and efficient food producer on any soil suitable for general garden crops.

Does the potato have a place in your home vegetable garden? The answer depends on the size of the garden.

On the average, a 100-foot row planted with 10 pounds of seed should yield between 1 and 2 bushels of potatoes. Obviously the 10 to 20 bushels a family of 5 might require for winter use would be difficult to produce in the small backyard garden. Yet, even in small gardens—after space has been provided for such vegetables as tomatoes, green beans, and leafy greens—the potato might be considered for planting on any remaining space.

Space-saving techniques such as intercropping can also be used in growing early potatoes in the small garden. Vining crops like cucumbers, melons and squash can be planted between rows of potatoes. After the early potatoes are harvested the area is free for the vine crops to spread and produce their crop.

The potato's home is in the mountainous regions of South America, although it is referred to as the Irish potato. It was cultivated rather extensively by the Inca Indians of Peru as far back as 200 A.D. Early explorers after Columbus introduced the potato to Europe between 1532 and 1550.

Not until the potato was introduced into Ireland was it recognized for its great food value rather than as a curiosity, and by the 1600's it was cultivated extensively in that country. For approximately 250 years the potato was a major source of food in most of Europe. In fact the majority of the population in Ireland depended on this crop for its existence.

When the late blight disease came from America into Ireland (1845-1847) it caused a national disaster. Destruction of the vines and decay of the tubers caused a complete loss of the crop nationwide. The result was the Irish famine in which thousands starved to death.

A colony of Presbyterian Irish who settled in New Hampshire introduced the potato to our country in 1719. Soon after the Irish famine the potato gained in importance in the United States.

As late as 1771 only two varieties of potato were listed, but during the 19th century thousands of varieties were developed and introduced in America. Only a small number were accepted, however. Some varieties still prominent today originated during that period. They include Irish Cobbler (1875), Russet Burbank (1876), Green Mountain (1878), Red McClure (1880), and White Rose (1893).

The cultivated potato in North America and Europe is known botanically as Solanam tuberosum. It is a member of the nightshade family which includes such plants as tomato, egg plant, pepper, ground cherry, bittersweet, petunia and tobacco.

Although grown as an annual, it is often considered a perennial because of its ability to reproduce vegetatively by means of tubers that arise from

Orrin C. Turnquist is Professor and Extension Horticulturist, University of Minnesota, St. Paul.

underground stems. In fact the tubers have all the characteristics of normal stems, including dormant true buds which are called eyes and rudimentary leaf scars that are called eyebrows.

The small dots on the tubers are identical to lenticels on a stem which facilitate the exchange of gases. These lenticels often become enlarged and objectionable when tubers develop in soils with excessive moisture and access of air is restricted.

Contrary to much common opinion, development of tubers does not depend upon flowering. Potato plants will form tubers without any flower development on top. The fruits or seed balls that develop from the flowers on some varieties are true fruits. These berries are not edible. They are not the result of cross pollination with the tomato, as many gardeners believe.

Although some of these fruits are seedless, normally they contain many small true seeds, no two of which are alike. The fact that these true seeds will not be the same as the variety from which they came is the reason we do not grow potatoes from true seed. Instead we propagate the potato by stem cuttings called seed pieces or seed eyes. The use of true seed is impractical for all except potato breeders who control the pollination and use the resulting seed in development of new varieties.

The tubers usually initiate at the tips of the stolons (underground stems) from 5 to 7 weeks after planting or when the plants are 6 to 8 inches tall. This varies with the variety and several environmental factors. As the plant grows the leaves make food for continuing growth. A point is reached, however, where a supply of food is made beyond what is needed for growth. This is when excess food is moved down into tubers for storage.

Environmental factors such as long

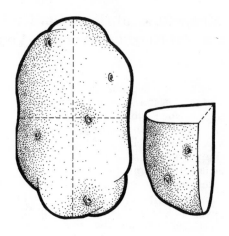

days, warm temperatures, high moisture and fertility tend to favor plant development whereas short days, cool temperatures, lower moisture, and less fertility promote tuber development. Don't forget that a good yield of potato tubers depends first of all upon a good healthy plant development.

Certified Seed

One of the most important steps to success in growing potatoes is the use of sound, healthy, certified seed. Potatoes are subject to several diseases whose symptoms are not easily recognized on either tubers or plants. Many are virus diseases that dwarf the plant and cut the yield in half. High-yielding seedstocks can be maintained only under carefully controlled conditions of isolation, disease control and storage.

Certified seed potatoes are grown mainly in the Northern States where lower growing temperatures favor the expression of virus disease symptoms so the infected plants can be eliminated. There are also fewer insects present that spread the diseases.

Potatoes are grown from "seed pieces" or "seed eyes" that are a quarter cut of the potato and include a couple of "eyes."

Home-produced potatoes may become infected in a single season, so there is no assurance that seed saved from a high yielding crop will perform satisfactorily the following year. It is best to buy new certified seed each year. Certified seed potatoes are usually identified by an official State Department of Agriculture tag on each bag. The higher cost of this seed is more than justified by the higher yield and better quality of the new crop.

Table stock potatoes that you buy at the food store should not be used for seed. They often have virus diseases present and may have been treated with a growth-inhibiting chemical to prevent them from sprouting in the market place.

Varieties

Many varieties of potatoes are certified in the United States each year. Some are more specific in their adaptability to certain regions than others. Furthermore, these varieties have a wide range of maturity from very early to late.

For the small garden, choose potato varieties that are early in maturity. This facilitates intercropping with some of the later vegetables that require more room further into the season after the potatoes have been harvested. For the larger garden the midseason and late varieties can be grown.

Potato varieties adapted to the home garden are:

Norland: A very early red variety with oblong, smooth tubers with shallow eyes. It has moderate resistance to common scab and good table quality. It is widely adapted and commonly available in the United States.

Irish Cobbler: An early maturity white variety with round to blocky tubers and deep eyes. It is a good producer and has excellent table quality. It is very susceptible to common scab.

Norgold: An early maturing russet variety with very smooth long to oblong tubers and shallow eyes. It is scab-resistant. Cooking quality is good, but under stressed growing conditions tubers could develop hollow heart.

Anoka: A newer early white variety with round to oval smooth uniform tubers. It is an all purpose potato well adapted to the home garden at 14-inch spacing. It has less tendency to darkening after cooking.

Superior. A midseason white variety with a rather tough skin. It is moderately resistant to scab and has high table quality.

Kennebec: A very popular late variety with white skin and shallow eyes. It has resistance to late blight disease. Cooking quality is excellent. Because of the thin skin the tubers are very susceptible to sunburn and greening.

Red Pontiac: A high yielding red variety with a midseason maturity. Tubers are oblong with medium deep eyes. Wih excessive moisture the tubers tend to become oversized. Cooking quality is only fair, but it is a good variety for winter storage.

Red LaSoda: A good red variety for gardens in the South. It is midseason in maturity with round to oblong tubers. Eyes are medium deep. It appears to have some tolerance to higher temperatures.

Katahdin: A very popular white variety with wide adaptability. Tubers are round to oblong with shallow eyes. It is midseason to late in maturity. Cooking quality is good.

Sebago: A late maturing white variety with resistance to late blight. It is popular in the South as well as in the East as a home garden variety. Tubers are smooth and nearly round with shallow eyes. Cooking quality is fair to good, but not as mealy as Kennebec.

Russet Burbank: Also known as Netted Gem and Idaho Russet. It is a late variety with long cylindrical to slightly flattened tubers with a heavily netted skin. Under conditions of moisture stress the tubers often develop growth cracks or knobs. It has some scab resistance. Table quality is excellent, especially for baking. Better size is obtained with a 14- to 16-inch spacing.

Consult the local extension service for new potato introductions with specific adaptation to your area. Potato breeders continue to develop varieties with improved market and culinary quality combined with high yield and multiple disease resistance.

Soil Needs

Like most vegetable crops, the potato is adapted to a wide variety of soils. It performs best, however, on a sandy loam well supplied with organic matter and plant food. High organic soils like peat or muck can be used if they are well drained. Heavy fine-textured soils are satisfactory if their structure is improved with organic matter.

Applying organic matter in the form of well-rotted manure, compost or similar materials will improve the structure for better air-holding capacity as well as water-holding capacity. Apply it to the top of the soil in early spring at the rate of 3 to 4 bushels per 100 square feet of area. With a rotary tiller, or spading fork, incorporate it thoroughly into the soil to make a uniform tilth or structure. This practice binds together coarse-textured sandy soils and breaks up fine-textured, heavy clay soils.

The best soil-acidity range for potatoes is between pH 4.8 to 5.4. On soils with a pH of 5.5 to 7.0 the potatoes usually are scabby. Lime should not be used unless a soil test indicates a pH below 4.8.

One of the most widely used commercial fertilizers for the home garden is 5-10-5. Another is 10-10-10. These analyses should provide suffi-

cient plant food for a good potato crop. Either fertilizer can be spread at the rate of 15 pounds per 1,000 square feet at planting time.

Some gardeners prefer to place the fertilizer in bands below and slightly to the side of seed pieces. If the rows are 3 feet apart and 100 feet long, apply 6 to 8 pounds per row. A side dressing may be applied after the plants are 4 to 6 inches high. Use the same rate in an open trench 4 inches deep and 6 inches away from the plants.

Local agricultural extension offices will have more specific recommendations for your area; however, the suggestions given here should generally be adequate.

Manure is often used as a source of nutrients where scab is not a problem. This disease is more serious when fresh manure is used. Manure that is well-rotted or applied during fall or early winter is less apt to increase potato scab.

Rotate the location of potatoes in your garden each year. At least a 3-year rotation is suggested for all garden crops. In large gardens where space is not limited it helps to plant a small grain such as rye as a nurse crop seeded down to red clover the second year. After the hay is cut the third year, the plot can be plowed down and fallowed. Potatoes are then planted in the area the fourth year. Such a rotation will help control diseases, insects and weeds. Potato yield and quality will be improved.

Planting

The potato is considered a cool-season crop and can be planted as soon as frost is out of the ground and the soil dry enough to work. If soil temperature is below 40° F (5° C), however, there is a greater chance for seed piece decay, especially when cut seed is planted. Using whole seed or cut seed that has been suberized will help prevent the problem. This is a process of healing over the cut surface by holding the cut seed for a period of 7 to 10 days at a temperature of 60° to 70° F (16° to 21° C) and a relative humidity of 85 percent with good air circulation.

Planting dates will vary with the locality and soil type. In the North, potatoes usually are planted from April 15 to May 15, and in the South from November to February.

Plant early to get the highest yield. By planting early maturing varieties as soon as the soil is dry enough to prepare and warm enough to prevent seed decay, you can have potatoes of usable size by midsummer. These will not keep as long as potatoes that matured later in the growing season, however.

Proper size of the seed piece planted is important. Experience has shown that 1½- to 2-ounce seed pieces are best. This is about the size of an average hen's egg. The so-called "potato eyes" are generally too small to provide sufficient nourishment, and as a result weak plants develop. Potatoes can be planted either whole or cut. If cut, there should be at least one eye on each piece and the pieces should be uniform and blocky.

Plant the seed immediately after cutting, otherwise viability will be lowered by loss of moisture and entrance of rot organisms.

Some gardeners prefer to treat seed potatoes before planting. A good fungicide dust such as captan will help protect the cut seed pieces after planting and assure better emergence.

Seed can be cut and stored for 10 days or more if it is properly suberized.

If available, whole B-size seed is best. The value of planting small potatoes without cutting them has been known in Europe for many years. With the skin around the entire potato, it is protected from soil organisms and the result is less seed decay and better stands of plants.

If whole or B-size seed is used, it should be from certified stock. Virus-infected plants tend to produce smaller tubers, and when such seed is planted whole, weak and poor yielding plants result. However, small tubers from certified seed will produce as good a crop as large potatoes cut for seed.

Plant potatoes deep enough so the new tubers will develop sufficiently beneath the surface to avoid sunburning. Generally the seed should be planted in contact with moist soil, 3 to 4 inches deep. This depth will vary with the soil's temperature and moisture. A shallow covering of about 2 to 3 inches of soil over the seed will result in quicker emergence and less sprout damage from rhizoctonia and blackleg disease.

In the small garden a trench is usually opened with a hand hoe or cultivator. Distance between rows will depend on the type of cultivation to be used. A 36-inch row is quite common, but rows can be spaced 24 inches apart if cultivated by hand. Within the trench, place the seed pieces 12 to 18 inches apart, depending on variety. Oversize potatoes in varieties like Kennebec can be prevented by planting seed pieces as close as 6 to 8 inches. This also helps reduce the amount of hollow heart in tubers.

The amount of seed needed varies with the spacing and size of the seed piece. When cut to a 1½-ounce size and planted 12 inches apart in the trench, a 100-foot row would require about 9 pounds of seed potatoes.

Water when dry periods occur, but only if the soil needs it. Once watering is begun it should be continued until the soil is moistened to an 8- to 12-inch depth. Water thoroughly at weekly intervals when needed. Dry periods alternating with wet periods can cause potatoes to develop such abnormalties as hollow heart, growth cracks, and knobs.

Pest Control

Cultivate frequently from planting time on, to destroy weeds in the seedling stages. When the plants first emerge, rake lightly over the row as well as between rows. All cultivation should be shallow—2 inches or less —to prevent pruning the potato roots near the surface. Hill or ridge the soil over the rows only if the tubers become exposed. This will help prevent sunburn and frost damage. Cease all cultivation when the vines fill in between the rows.

A pre-emergence weed killer is registered for use in many vegetable crops, including potatoes. When used according to label directions, it is very good for control of annual broadleaved weeds and grasses. Another herbicide applied to the garden in the fall after harvest is an excellent treatment for quackgrass. It is not selective but will kill perennial grasses when applied as directed on the label. Plowing or rototilling can be deferred until spring with no residual effect on potatoes or other vegetables to be planted in the treated area.

Numerous insect and disease pests may attack potatoes. An ounce of prevention is worth a pound of cure. Use certified seed as a fundamental step in disease control. Practicing a 3- to 4-year rotation in the garden will help prevent both insect and disease problems.

Soil insects troublesome to potatoes are white grubs, wireworms and cutworms. Most garden soil insecticides give satisfactory control.

You can control leaf-feeding insects like the Colorado potato beetle and the flea beetle with recommended chemicals. Control leaf-sucking insects like leaf hoppers and aphids with a contact insecticide.

Prevent foliage diseases such as late blight and early blight by applying recommended fungicides every 7 to 10 days according to label directions. Several new materials are available for disease control. Soil-borne diseases such as scab and verticillium wilt may be reduced by growing resistant varieties and following a good rotation.

Any damage to potato plants—by insects, disease or other causes—will result in an abnormal crop of poor quality. The better the plant growth, the better the crop of potatoes.

Harvest, Storage

Potatoes may be harvested once the tubers are large enough. As long as the vines remain alive, the size of the potatoes and the yield will continue to increase. When the vines are completely dead and the skin ceases to slip from pressure by the thumb, the potatoes can be dug with a spading fork or plow.

Avoid bruises or other injuries such as cuts and fork holes in digging and handling. Do not expose the freshly-dug potatoes to sun or wind as they are very susceptible to scald and sunburn at that time. Potatoes have a sweating period the first two weeks after harvest. During this time they

Flea beetle that causes damage to many garden plants is not much larger than a flea and jumps like one when disturbed.

Potatoes are very sensitive to light, which causes green pigment to develop under the skin in the flesh of the tuber. This will make them bitter and unfit for table use. Tubers that have an excessive amount of greening should be discarded. If greening is only slight the affected area can be peeled away before use. Always keep potatoes in a place with total darkness to avoid greening in storage.

If the temperature in the storage room reaches 32° F (0° C), the potatoes often become sweet. Increasing the temperature for a few days will cause the sugar to revert to starch and good table quality will be restored.

should be kept in a place where the temperature is about 65° F (18° C) and the relative humidity at 85% to 95%. This will help the healing-over of any injuries or wounds in harvest.

Sort over the potatoes and place only the best, sound tubers in bins or containers for winter storage. Store them dry in a room that can be kept at a temperature of 35° to 40° F (2° to 5° C) and a moderate humidity. Under these conditions well-matured tubers will keep in good condition for 7 to 8 months. Above 40° F (5° C) they may keep for 2 to 3 months but sprouting and shriveling may occur.

Sprout-inhibiting chemicals are available under various trade names from garden supply stores. A common type is applied to the vines according to label directions during the growing season. The harvested tubers are safe for table use and they will not sprout when kept at higher storage temperatures such as found in a modern basement room.

Some people have developed the erroneous idea that potatoes are fattening, but studies show this is not true. Potatoes are less fattening pound for pound than most foods in the daily American diet. The potato alone is comparatively low in calories per pound, but when fried or served with a lot of butter or sour cream the caloric intake may be high. French fried potatoes have about five times the caloric value as the same weight of mashed potatoes.

Besides being a good source of food energy, the potato is also a source of iron, thiamin, niacin, and vitamin C.

A few rows of potatoes in the home garden properly planted and well cared for should provide satisfaction and achievement as well as some nutritious food to enjoy at your table.

Harvesting potatoes in the home garden — "it's a good feeling."

Sweet Potatoes—Buried Treasure

by John C. Bouwkamp

Since most of us will never savor the excitement of digging for buried treasure, digging sweet potatoes in your garden may be the next best thing. The day-by-day progress of your crop of tomatoes and beans is readily apparent but the reward for your efforts with sweet potatoes must await the day of harvest. Variety names such as Jewel, Goldrush, Nugget, Nemagold, Gem, and Maryland Golden allude to the feeling of buried treasure by their developers.

The sweet potato, like many of our vegetable crops, originated in the Tropics. The exact area of origin is subject to debate but was probably in tropical America or somewhere in the tropical South Pacific islands. Two of the ancient civilizations of tropical America, the Mayan and the Peruvian, grew and cultivated sweet potatoes, although maize was their staple crop.

Primitive cultures of the South Pacific islands give a central role to the sweet potato in their celebrations, suggesting that sweet potatoes were culivated for food in two widely separated parts of the world from ancient times. Whether the crop originated in the New World and was transported to the Polynesian islands or vice versa remains open to speculation.

Although Columbus noted the use of sweet potatoes by West Indian natives on his fourth voyage, there is no record of pre-Columbian cultivation of sweet potatoes by Indians in the continental United States. Sweet potatoes were grown in Virginia as early as 1648, most likely from roots obtained in the West Indies.

A frequent source of confusion is use of the terms sweet potato and yam. The true yam (*Dioscorea* sp.) is of African or Chinese origin and belongs to a different plant family than the sweet potato. It is only rarely grown in the United States.

The Blacks, when first brought to this country, mistook the sweet potato for a type of yam since the sweet potato was unknown to them and the two crops grew and were used in a similar manner. Their word *nyami* was shortened to yam and the sweet potato became known as a yam in many parts of the United States, particularly in the South.

The terminology was further confused since the dry-fleshed varieties grown in the Middle States and North (known as sweet potatoes) were noticeably different from the moist-fleshed varieties grown in the Deep South (known as yams). Thus many people came to believe sweet potatoes and yams were different vegetables.

At present, the same varieties are grown throughout the United States and a sweet potato by any other name is still the tasty, nutritious vegetable many people associate with holidays and special meals.

Almost everyone knows that sweet potatoes are a delicious addition to any meal, but not many know they also are very nutritious. An average sized boiled sweet potato (2-inch diameter, 5 inches long) will provide over half the recommended daily allowance (RDA) of Vitamin C and more than twice the RDA of Vitamin A for an adult male, 23 to 55 years old and weighing 154 pounds.

In addition, this root will provide nearly 5% of the protein, 6% of the calcium, 9% of the phosphorous, 11% of the iron, 10% of the thiamin, 5% of the niacin and nearly 6% of the riboflavin required by an adult male.

John C. Bouwkamp is an Associate Professor of Horticulture at the University of Maryland, College Park.

All these vitamins and minerals are provided with about 170 calories (6.4% of the RDA). Empty calories? Not sweet potatoes!

Growing Requirements

What will you need to know about growing sweet potatoes?

First, sweet potatoes are a tropical crop and need 4 to 5 frost-free months for growing. They thrive in hot weather. Probably little or no growth occurs when soil or air temperatures are below 60° F. Growth appears to be optimum when soil temperatures are near 70° and air temperatures near 85°.

Second, since the root is the part you will harvest, the soil should be loose and friable (crumbly)—allowing for unimpeded root enlargement and easy digging.

Meet these two requirements, and you should be a success as a grower.

Choose a well-drained site in the full sun. The pH should be in the range of 5.5 to 6.5. If your garden is moderately fertile, apply 3½ pounds of 5-10-20 (or a similar analysis) of fertilizer per 100 feet of row before ridge construction or transplanting. If your garden is very sandy and/or infertile, 5 pounds per 100 feet would be more appropriate. If it's very rich and fertile, 2 to 2½ pounds should suffice.

Allan Stoner

In many parts of the country, sweet potatoes are grown on ridges 8 to 15 inches high. These are especially important on heavy or poorly drained soils. If the soil remains water logged for several days, the roots may rot. Ridges are a good idea if this is likely to occur.

If your garden is a fine sandy loam and well drained, probably no ridge is necessary.

Should you wish to grow on ridges, construct them before transplanting. Rows should be 3 to 4 feet apart.

Plan to obtain disease-free plants, also called sprouts, from a reputable dealer. Your choice of varieties differs widely in various parts of the United States, and not all varieties will be available at any location. Your local Extension Office would be your best choice for help in choosing a variety.

You may also wish to produce your own sprouts after you have some experience with growing sweet potatoes. Set plants 2 to 3 inches deep, and 12 to 16 inches apart in the rows, one plant per hill. Don't transplant until soil temperature reaches 60° F. A good rule of thumb is to plant sweet potatoes 1 to 2 weeks after frost danger is past.

After transplanting you may wish to water the plants with ½ cup or more of water or ½ cup of a starter solution. Starter solution can be made by mixing ½ ounce of a soluble, high phosphorus fertilizer (15-30-15 or similar analysis) per gallon of water. Be careful not to overdo the starter solution or you may damage the plants.

Hoe and cultivate sweet potatoes frequently (once per week) after the vines have begun to run. This serves two purposes—to control the weeds and to keep the vines from rooting at the nodes. If these nodes are al-

Vigorous growth of young sweet potato vines.

213

lowed to root, some storage roots may develop and the main storage roots will not develop as quickly.

Three to four weeks after transplanting, make a second application of fertilizer at the same rate as before transplanting. Place the fertilizer near the rows and work it into the soil.

After 6 to 8 weeks the vines will become too large to cultivate and you must weed by hand.

Moisture Needs

Once established, sweet potatoes

Allan Stoner

Sweet potatoes at harvest.

may be considered drought-hardy, and will produce a fair crop even under quite dry conditions. But supply them with ample moisture for best yields. They need about ¾ inch of rain or irrigation per week while small, and up to 2 inches of water per week when growing vigorously in hot weather.

Occasional leaf wilting during the hot part of the day is no cause for concern. But if the plants do not revive by early evening, you may wish to irrigate.

Excessive moisture after a prolonged dry period may cause the roots to crack. These cracks usually heal over by harvest time, resulting in a less appealing appearance but with no loss to eating or storing quality.

Sweet potatoes do not ripen or mature, so the time for harvest is judged by root size. At about 110 to 120 days after transplanting (if you can wait that long) you may wish to check on root size. To do so, carefully dig away some of the soil from several hills near the center of the row— the end plants may develop faster. When a majority of the roots have reached a size you desire, they should be dug immediately. A light frost which only slightly damages the vines won't cause problems.

Dig roots carefully to avoid injury. A shovel usually works better than a fork. After digging, place the roots in containers. Keep separate any badly injured or cut roots for immediate use.

A yield of two pounds a plant is good.

Optimum conditions for curing and storing sweet potatoes are rather exact and should be maintained as nearly as possible. ("Curing" is a means of preparing sweet potatoes for storage.) Cure roots 6 to 8 days at about 85° F and 85% to 90% relative humidity. Temperatures should never exceed 90°. A high relative humidity can best be maintained by loosely wrapping the containers in polyethylene film. Don't cure in the sun as the roots may sunburn.

After curing, store the roots in a cool place (55° to 60° F) with a high relative humidity (85%). An unheated area of the basement or a root cellar might be okay.

If storage temperatures drop below 50° F for an extended time, chilling injury may develop and the roots may spoil. Temperatures above 65° will likely result in sprouting and pithiness. If the relative humidity is too low, shriveling will result. However, if proper conditions are maintained you may expect your sweet potatoes to keep well and provide good eating through winter and into spring.

If you wish to produce your own "seed" for the following year, begin when the plants have developed vines 1½ to 2 feet long. Cut a segment 8 to 10 inches long from the tip of a vine and transplant it into a row which has been fertilized as previously mentioned. Plants should be set about a foot apart and 2 to 3 inches deep, making sure to cover at least 1 node. Water with ½ cup of starter solution or water.

You can expect a 10-fold increase with most varieties. So if you want 100 plants next year, have 10 hills of vine cuttings. Fertilize and cultivate your cuttings as suggested for the regular crop.

If the majority of roots from the vine cuttings are 1 inch in diameter or larger, harvest them at the same time as your main crop. Roots produced for sprouts should be cured and stored the same way as roots for table use.

Producing Sprouts

If you have produced roots from vine cuttings and wish to produce your own sprouts, several methods may be used depending upon the facilities at hand. If a heated frame is available, place disease-free "seed" roots near each other but not touching, and cover them with 1½ to 2 inches of light sand 4 to 5 weeks before transplanting. Soil temperature should not exceed 85° F. Open the sash on warm sunny days to avoid excessive heat buildup.

When the sprouts are 6 inches tall (usually a week or two before transplanting) turn off the heat and leave the sash open, except for very cold nights. Water the bed as necessary to keep it damp but not waterlogged.

Alternatively, you may wish to bed roots in a cold frame. Put your cold frame in a sunny place protected from wind. Allow an extra week to produce sprouts without heat, but otherwise the procedure is about the same.

If neither a cold frame nor a heated bed is available, you can bed sweet potatoes in your garden. Choose a sunny spot protected from wind and make a raised bed 6 to 8 inches high and 1½ to 2 feet wide, 6 to 7 weeks before transplanting. Bed the roots as described and cover with 1½ to 2 inches of sand. Then cover the bed with clear polyethylene film, securely anchoring edges of the plastic with soil.

When the sprouts begin to emerge, ventilate the plastic by punching ¼-inch holes every 6 to 8 inches. After 2 to 3 weeks or when the sprouts are 3 to 4 inches tall, you may remove the plastic—but replace it if a frost is likely. The sprouts should be 6 to 8 inches tall by transplanting time.

Remove sprouts from the roots by grasping them firmly one at a time and pulling sharply from the soil. With a little practice you should be able to pull sprouts without disturbing the bedded root. Transplant the sprouts as soon as possible. The bedded roots will continue to produce sprouts which may be used for a second planting, or you may wish to dig up the roots and destroy them.

Fortunately for the home gardener, there are relatively few serious disease and insect pests of sweet potatoes. Fusarium wilt, also called blue stem and stem rot, attacks certain varieties resulting in both a loss of plants and a yield reduction. It can be best controlled by growing resistant varieties and a rotation of four or more years' duration.

Scurf, also called soil stain, causes a dark "freckled" appearance to the skin of storage roots. The fungus attacks only the skin and causes no loss to eating quality. Control it by using only vine cuttings to produce the "seed" roots.

Pox or soil rot results in deep corky pits on the root. Once again, although the appearance is greatly affected, eating quality is not. Control pox by reducing the soil pH to 5.0 to 5.5, resulting in greatly reduced incidence and severity.

Black rot is occasionally a problem both in the garden and in storage. Affected areas begin as small black, nearly round spots, but under favorable conditions they enlarge and may nearly cover the root and extend well into the flesh. Usually you can control it by using disease-free sprouts, not planting in the same area of your garden each year, and using clean containers for storage. Some fungicides are effective in controlling black rot.

Rhizopus rot or soft rot attacks the roots after harvest, usually entering through a wound. It results in total loss of the root. Control soft rot by carefully handling the roots during harvesting, thus avoiding as much as possible any injury to them, and by curing the roots properly as soon after harvest as possible in order to heal wounds.

Fusarium root rot or surface rot is usually not noticed until after some months of storage. It appears as a generally circular spot, black or dark brown, sometimes slightly sunken, and only extends about ⅛ inch into the root's flesh. If infected areas are pared away the remainder of the root may be eaten. There is no known means of control, but immediate and proper curing helps in reducing the incidence. The occurrence is sporadic and seldom reaches serious proportions.

Nematodes may cause serious losses to sweet potato yields. The infected roots become misshapen and cracked, and galls may be observed on feeder roots. At present the home gardener has no effective way to control nematodes. Many varieties are resistant to one or more races or species of nematodes. Your local Extension Office is the best source of information if nematodes become a problem.

Although several species of insects and soil grubs attack sweet potatoes, they rarely result in serious losses. Damage is usually confined to a small area of a root and may be pared away prior to cooking. If serious losses occur, consult your Extension Office.

I have tried to outline the how's and why's of sweet potato growing for the average gardener, but experience is the best teacher. You may find it advisable to change some of the recommendations.

Sweet potatoes are likely to produce a fair crop even if you make a few mistakes, so feel free to experiment with changes after you have a little experience. If you fail in your attempt to grow sweet potatoes, find out why and try again. After all, not everyone finds buried treasure on their first try.

Herbs for Flavor, Fragrances, Fun In Gardens, Pots, in Shade, in Sun

by Doris Thain Frost

Herbs give much pleasure and profit if you grow them yourself. Plant herbs in your garden, read books about them, and discover personal joy and an added dimension to your cooking.

First of all, a place is needed to plant the seeds or roots and this means productive soil. A grower with an outdoor plot is indeed fortunate. Herbs will grow well in any garden where vegetables thrive, in the garden rows or around the edges. Herbs will grow in flower beds, in borders, among ornamental shrubs and roses, just so there is good drainage and six or more hours of sun.

Most herbs prefer an alkaline soil, a pH of 6.5 to 7.5. If the soil test indicates acidity, work ground limestone into the soil. The amount will be indicated in the soil test analysis received from your county extension services.

If an outdoor plot is lacking, many herbs will grow in boxes, pots or hanging baskets if the same conditions—good soil, drainage and sun—exist.

When planning an herb garden, remember that herbs belong in different classes according to their life span. Annuals, tender and hardy, may be planted in the vegetable garden as they mature in one season. Biennials and tender and hardy perennials must be planted in locations that will not be disturbed by cultivation or rotation as they live several years.

Prepare the plot as for vegetables.

Doris Thain Frost of Great Falls, Va., is a board member of the Herb Society of America, has taught herb classes at the National Arboretum, and is editor of the *Garden Bulletin* issued by the National Capital Area Federation of Garden Clubs.

Animal manure and compost are good fertilizers, preferably applied in early spring. Use mulches to keep the herb foliage clean, for weed control, and to preserve soil moisture. Cocoa hulls, buckwheat hulls, leaves, straw and hay are popular mulches.

Herbs are propagated by seeds, cuttings, layering, and divisions. If you want only a few plants, buy them from commercial growers.

Seeds come in packets sold by established seed houses and by some commercial herb growers. Unless you have the equipment and space to start seeds indoors to transplant later, experience has proven that the average gardener had best buy seeds of annuals and plant them where they are to grow, and start perennials from cuttings, divisions and plants.

Parsley, the culinary biennial, can be started from seed if many plants are desired, or a few small plants purchased.

Cuttings can be rooted in water or in a medium of perlite, milled sphagnum moss, or in compressed peat pellets. The rooted cuttings may be transplanted into pots or into the garden if the season permits.

Divisions are made by digging up an older plant and pulling apart or cutting sections of the root and replanting each section individually.

Plants from commercial growers should be carefully examined for insects and disease, and if they are to grow outdoors, bought and planted when the ground has warmed and all danger of frost is past.

Bees, lady bugs, praying mantis and many other insects are friends in the herb garden as they pollinate plants and also destroy insect enemies. Herbs are peculiarly resistant to most insects and diseases.

Sometimes mints become mildewy early in the season. Either harvest early, or cut and destroy the affected stems. New growth for the second crop will be free of mildew.

Sometimes dill and fennel attract tomato worms. These can be removed by hand. Japanese beetles attack basil. Shake them off into a can of kerosene or into a bucket with warm water, salt and detergent added.

Do not use poisonous substances or powders on any herb to be used in food or beverages.

When to Harvest

The secret of a good harvest is timing, taking into account the readiness of the plant and the use to which it will be put. Just before the flowers fully open is said to be the time when the most oils and flavors are present and the richest fragrances prevail.

Successive harvests can be made of mints, comfrey, basils, parsley and others by cutting the stems early in the season, not too close to the ground so that new growth will start quickly. Cut again in late summer, and—with annuals—before frost when the entire plant may be harvested. If seeds are desired or self seeding is planned, a crop must be allowed to mature and ripen seeds.

Herbs for future use may be dried, frozen, the flavors preserved in vinegars and jellies, or kept fresh for a short time. To dry, cut the stems or stalks when the plant is ready, as I explained. Don't cut too close to the ground. Separate into small bunches, tie with string, and hang in a warm, dry, dark place such as an attic or vacant room until the leaves are crisp and brittle. In the summer this takes from three to ten days.

Strip the leaves, and buds or flowerettes if desired, and put as whole as possible into a jar with a tight lid. Check for a few days to be sure the herbs are perfectly dry, or mold, mildew or other problems will de-

velop. The leaves are kept as whole as possible to preserve the flavor. They can be crumbled when used.

When only the leaves are dried, as with comfrey, gather the leaves, and spread thinly on newspaper in a warm, dry place until crispy dry. Then store in jars.

Basil, parsley and chives sometimes turn very dark if air dried. Stems of these can be laid on brown paper and put into an oven at 150° F or less. Leave the oven door open to allow moisture to escape. This method takes several hours.

The quickest, most modern way is to dry in a microwave oven. Place sprigs on a paper towel and cover with a paper towel. Put into the oven for one minute. Take out of oven and cool. If not completely dry put back into oven for a few seconds. When crumbly, store in jars. Basil, sage, parsley, mints and oregano, especially, retain beautiful, appetizing green colors when dried this way.

If only seeds are to be used, such as from dill, fennel or coriander, take care to cut the stems when ripe but before the seeds fall. A paper bag carefully put over a head or umbel and tied with string before the head is severed is then hung upside down (seed head down) to catch the seeds as they dry and fall.

Freezing

To freeze herbs, gather as for drying, wash if dusty, pat off excess water, place into plastic bags and put into the freezer immediately. When it's time to use them, snip or chop the herbs without thawing as they mince easily while frozen. Mint, tarragon, lovage, parsley, chives, sorrel, and sweet marjoram take kindly to this method.

Another good way to freeze is to put the chopped herbs into an ice cube tray, fill with water, and freeze. Then put the cubes into plastic bags and store in the freezer. The cubes can easily be popped into soups or stews when needed.

Herb flavors can be enjoyed in vinegars, jellies, and pickles.

Fresh herbs are probably the most desired as the flavor is at its best. Herbs can be kept in the vegetable bin of a refrigerator for a while, at least through the winter holidays. Or they may be planted in pots and kept in a sunny place or in a greenhouse.

Parsley, chives, sweet marjoram, thyme and basil are some of the easiest to grow in pots. Many herbs have deep or large root systems that require more space than is usually available in pots.

Herbs that are easy to grow and delightful to use are listed below. Do try to grow some of them in your home garden. Advanced herbalists will know many more.

BASIL—*Ocimum basilicum* (pronounced like dazzle). A tender annual. Plant seeds when all danger of frost is past, and cut the last harvest before cold winds turn the leaves black. Of the many varieties, lettuce leaf, dwarf bush, lemon, and the purple or opal basils are the ones used for flavoring food.

Harvest basil when the flower heads appear. If the leaves are to be kept growing, keep the flower heads pinched out. Use fresh in salads, salad dressing, soups, and vegetables. Basil's clove-like flavor has a special affinity for tomatoes, cottage cheese, and egg dishes. The leaves can be dried quickly in the oven, or made into a vinegar to which the red or opal variety gives a lovely ruby color.

CHIVES — *Allium schoenoprasum* is the most delicate tasting member of the onion family (see onion chapter for production details). The tender, hollow spears are cut and chopped finely to flavor a great variety of dishes.

The lavender flower heads of chives may be cut close to the ground and dried to go in winter arrange-

Glenn M. Christiansen

ments, or chopped fresh and added to salad. A beautiful perennial, chives often are grown as garden borders.

Chives are best used fresh, and a fresh supply can be kept for winter by potting a few plants and bringing them indoors in fall. Or the snipped foliage may be frozen in ice cubes as described before.

Chives are good in herb butters, green salads, in sour cream for dressing potatoes, in fact in any dish where a mild onion flavor is desired.

DILL—*Anethum graveolens* is a hardy annual. Plant the seeds where they are to grow in the early spring, or in the autumn to get an early start. Make successive plantings from April to July. Dill reseeds very easily if a few plants are allowed to mature.

Both fresh foliage and seeds of dill are used in pickling, in vinegar, minced over salads, cottage cheese and potatoes, blended into sauces for veal and fish, or baked into dilly bread. Dill foliage is the dill weed found in the grocery store.

Fresh-picked dill grown indoors makes sandwich garnish.

219

Dill has such a refreshing flavor that it should be much more widely used. Green dill umbels are distinctive in flower arrangements.

EGYPTIAN ONION—*Allium cepa* var. *vivaparum* is a hardy perennial, a curious member of the onion family that forms its bulbs on the tips of its long green shoots rather than in the ground, as most of its relatives do. (See onion chapter for production details.)

Egyptian onion is a very ornamental plant in a garden border. The bulbs may be used in any way an ordinary onion is used. The fresh stalks may be chopped and used too.

GARLIC—*Allium sativum.* Garlic's health-giving qualities have been known since ancient times. It also serves as a bug repellent in the garden. (See onion chapter for production details.)

Garlic gives that extra touch to a salad, pickles, and vegetables. The taste for it develops and often it is used as a condiment at the table like salt and pepper. Garlic contains an important essential oil, allicin. Chewing a sprig of parsley or a whole clove is supposed to sweeten the breath after indulging in garlic-flavored food.

Garlic butter is excellent with sour dough or French bread, and garlic vinegar for flavoring potato salad, stews, and cooked greens.

LOVAGE—*Levisticum officinale* is a hardy perennial that often grows to six feet in height. Plant it in a permanent place as it lives many years. One or two plants are enough for a small garden. It grows from seed but the best way to begin is with a division from an old plant, or with a young plant from a nursery.

Lovage likes a bit of shade and moisture. The large celery-like leaves are the usable parts. They have a strong celery flavor. The leaves can be cut from the stems and put fresh in salads and soups, or like celery used with other vegetables. In the fall, the leaves can be spread out to dry on paper for winter use.

The dried leaves turn yellowish and do not keep their flavor much more than a year. All the foliage will die down in the fall but new shoots appear in early spring. Lovage is ornamental in a garden corner.

SWEET MARJORAM—*Marjorana hortensis* is a tender perennial, treated as an annual. It is sometimes called knotted marjoram because of the form of the flowers and seeds along the stem ends. It is a small, low plant, most easily started by buying plants and setting them into the garden when the ground is warm. Seeds may be sown indoors in early spring and transplanted later but this is for the advanced gardener.

Two harvests may be made. The first is when the plant starts to bloom. Cut back all the stems, leaving at least an inch of the stems above ground. The harvested marjoram may be dried in small bunches or spread on paper

M. S. Lowman

A pot marjoram.

in a warm, dry room. The plants can be cut again when they flower the second time.

Culinary uses are many, as marjoram is one of the most aromatic herbs. The delicious, spicy flavor remains when the leaves are dried. It can be used with fowl, lamb, herb butters, vegetables, and in herbal tea mixtures.

MINTS—*Mentha*. There are many varieties of these hardy perennials. The most popular mints are peppermint (of which curly mint is a variety), spearmint, and orange and apple mint. The best way to start is to find a friend who has a mint bed and get one or two root divisions, or buy them from a nursery.

Mint likes moist, fertile soil and doesn't mind some shade. It reproduces by sending long, lateral stolons (runners) under the ground. These may be divided to supply new plants.

Mints may be cut two or three times each year, leaving a few inches of stem to grow again. The leaves are stripped off and dried in a warm dry place, or oven, or hung to dry in small bunches and stripped later.

You can make mint tea, mint sauces, mint jelly, or mix mint with other herbs or citrus juices for teas and jellies. The fresh leaves may be used in green or fruit salads, with new peas, and in candy.

OREGANO—*Origanum* has many varieties. These hardy perennials are not clearly defined by herbal authorities. The oreganos and marjorams are closely related but the varieties are different in growth and flavor.

Greek oregano, *Origanum heracleoticum,* is thought by some to be the true oregano. This plant is treated as a tender perennial in the Washington (D.C.) area. It is slow growing and the flowers are white.

Others call *Origanum vulgare,* a very hardy perennial, the true oregano. It grows several feet high. The blooms are pink and purplish.

Oreganos are propagated by cuttings, divisions, and young plants from nurseries—often not labeled correctly.

As soon as the flowers appear the stems may be cut to dry in small bunches. The leaves may be used fresh all summer long.

Oregano goes well with tomato dishes, tomato juice, pizzas and other pastas, spaghetti, macaroni, and noodles. It also enhances lamb, beef, soups, and salads.

PARSLEY—*Petroselinum hortense* is a very hardy biennial. The seeds take about three weeks to germinate, unless soaked overnight in water before planting. An old saying is that the seeds must go to the devil seven times and back before they will come up.

Busy gardeners usually buy plants from a nursery every year and plant them in a permanent plot or border in order to always have a good supply. The foliage makes an attractive low border. Medicinal uses of parsley are ancient and numerous since the plant is a rich source of vitamins A and C and of calcium, niacin riboflavin and other properties. Parsley is often made into an infusion or tea and drunk alone or combined with other herbs to promote health. The leaves are used for flavoring in soups, stews, potato dishes, and as a breath sweetener with garlic-seasoned dishes.

Harvest parsley by cutting the stems an inch or two above the ground, and dry quickly on paper in a dry, shady place as the leaves turn dark very easily. Many think oven methods are best to preserve color and flavor.

Fresh parsley can be used most of the year as it is very hardy. It is also lovely in hanging baskets for indoor gardens.

ROSEMARY—*Rosmarinus officinalis* is a tender evergreen perennial, one of the most esteemed and decorative herbs. It needs a well drained alkaline soil, a sunny location, and protection during the winter until well established. It makes a beautiful large pot plant in a green house.

Rosemary is propagated by cuttings or layering. Young plants may be bought from nurseries. Late summer is the best time to take cuttings.

Rosemary has an assertive spicy flavor delicious with lamb, chicken, other meat dishes and stuffings. Rosemary butter is luscious on hot biscuits. The tips and leaves may be dried for future use, but since the plant is evergreen, fresh tips are always available.

M. S. Lowman

SAGE—*Salvia officinalis* is a hardy evergreen perennial that becomes woody and sprawly after four or five years. Sage is most easily propagated from seeds or young plants from a nursery. It needs sun—and good drainage.

The fresh leaves may be used all year, but cuttings of sprigs may be dried in a warm shady place or by oven methods. Sage makes a good, healthful tea. Its strong, dominating flavor improves cheeses, poultry, dressings, sausages, pork, and wines.

SALAD BURNET—*Sanguisorba minor* is a hardy perennial easily grown from seed in full sun. As it grows 1 to 2 feet tall, it should be thinned to leave the plants 12 to 18 inches apart. The leaves are used fresh as the cucumbery taste and smell vanish when dried. It is a pretty border plant. The leaves are fern-like and usually evergreen. The flavor is good in fresh salads, vinegar, and wine punches.

SORREL, FRENCH—*Rumex scutatus* is a very hardy perennial, whose broad leaves add a nice sharp taste to spring greens, spinach, and herbal soups. It is used fresh. The leaves can be cut throughout the growing season. It is grown from seed or from root divisions. The flower stalks should be removed as they appear, so that the green leaves may be produced longer.

SUMMER SAVORY—*Satureia hortensis* is a hardy annual whose seeds are sown in the garden in the spring. It grows fast and the plants should be hilled to keep them upright. Savory needs sun and plenty of moisture.

Savory can be cut and dried when the flowers open, or the tips of the plants pinched and used fresh throughout the summer. Savory makes a delicate tea. It is the Bohnenkraut of the Germans, excellent with green beans, butters, spreads, green salads, egg dishes, and all kinds of meat.

Winter Savory, *Satureia montana*, is a hardy perennial that forms a small bush with lavender flowers. It is very desirable as a border plant, but not as aromatic as summer savory—therefore less useful in cooking.

TARRAGON—*Artemisia dracunculus* is a tender perennial, unless the roots are somewhat protected with straw or mulch during the winter in the Northeastern areas. Avoid buying seeds as the true variety rarely sets seeds—you might find you have the Russian or Siberian variety which is very vigorous but lacks the aromatic scent and flavor of the true type.

Tarragon plant at harvest stage. Leaves and tops may be cut several times during season.

Propagate from a cutting or root division or buy young plants from a reputable source. Plant in a sunny place, especially well drained, with room for the shallow lateral roots. Stems should be harvested in early summer, leaving at least three inches of stem above the ground to furnish growth for one or two more harvests later in the year.

Dry the leaves quickly as they turn brown easily. Try oven methods. When dry, seal in dry tight containers. A better idea is to pot a plant or two to keep indoors and enjoy fresh. Fertilize regularly and keep on the dry side.

The culinary uses of tarragon are ancient. Tarragon vinegar is well known for flavoring sauces and salad dressings. Tarragon is especially delectable on fish, cauliflower, spinach, roast turkey, and egg dishes, and it makes sauce Bearnaise. The robust flavor is best used alone and not combined with other herbs.

THYME—*Thymus vulgaris* is a hardy perennial that can be started from seed, but best results are from divisions or plants purchased from a nursery. Plant in a sunny, well drained location. It is a low, bushy plant with lovely blooms that is attractive in a foreground. Of the many varieties, the so-called French and English thymes are best for culinary purposes.

One cutting, made when the flowers begin to open, is taken for drying. The next growth should be left to help the plant survive the winter. Dry on paper in a warm, dry room. When dry, rub off the leaves and discard the stems. Store in dry, tight jars.

Thyme makes a stimulating tea and can be used to flavor any meat, fish, or vegetable. It is good in most any food. Greek thyme honey is famous. It can be found in organic food stores, or a thyme syrup can be made from our native honey mixed with strong thyme tea.

Basic Herbal Recipes

Herb Butter

Soften one half stick butter (sweet, unsalted if possible)

Add one tablespoon finely minced fresh herb or one-half teaspoon dried herb

Cream together, adding a few drops lemon juice

Use on hot breads, vegetables, baked potatoes

Herbs to use: basil, tarragon, thyme, chives, dill, parsley, marjoram, rosemary

Herb Vinegar

Clean and dry wide-mouthed glass jars

Gather fresh herbs. If dusty rinse in cold water and pat dry (water clouds vinegar)

Fill jar lightly with herbs

Heat, do *not* boil, good cider or wine vinegar

Pour vinegar over herb, cover with a non-rust lid or just put waxed paper over mouth of jar

Set jar in room temperature location for two or three weeks

Strain through cheesecloth and bottle

Herbs to use: dill, basil, salad burnet, tarragon, mint

Herb Jelly

Two cups herb infusion

One fourth cup vinegar or apple cider

Four and one half cups sugar

Heat the above until sugar is dissolved (high heat)

When boiling add one half bottle liquid pectin

Rolling boil for one and one half minutes

Take off fire. Add one or two drops food coloring if desired

Fill sterilized jelly glasses and seal with melted paraffin.

Herbs to use: Sage, basil, thyme, parsley, marjoram, rosemary, mint

Infusion: 2½ cups boiling water over 1 cup fresh herb. Let cool and strain

For Further Reading:

A Primer for Herb Growing, The Herb Society of America, 300 Massachusetts Ave., Boston, Mass. 02115. 50¢.

Foster, Gertrude B., *Herbs for Every Garden,* E. P. Dutton and Company, Inc., 201 Park Ave. S., New York, N. Y. 10003. $5.95.

Okra Is Produced Primarily in the South As Main Dish Vegetable, and for Gumbos

by W. D. Kimbrough, L. G. Jones, and J. F. Fontenot

Okra (*Abelmoschus esculentus* (L) Moench) is a member of the mallow family, closely related to Chinese hibiscus and to cotton. Its beginnings are uncertain, but it probably originated in Africa or Asia and was brought to America by the Spanish. Okra is a warm weather plant. Under ideal conditions a perennial, it is grown in the United States as an annual, since cold usually kills it here.

Grown extensively in home gardens in the South, okra is commonly served as a main dish vegetable. It can be used fresh or may be frozen or canned.

The immature seed pods, produced over a relatively long period if harvested regularly, are the edible part of the okra plant. Okra is especially important to the lower South, where not many vegetables are productive from midsummer through early fall. Most home gardens of the South should have a place for okra. However, in small gardens there may not be room, as the plants get fairly large and occupy the space for a long time.

Okra is grown to some extent in Northern gardens, but due to the shorter growing season the yields will not be as large as in the South.

Composition of okra pods varies somewhat with growing conditions and stage of maturity. The more immature the pods, the less food value they have. They consist mainly of water and carbohydrates, like most vegetables. Several vitamins and minerals also are present.

Okra contains mucilaginous material that some people object to, as it makes certain okra dishes seem slimy. This material, however, is what makes okra so desirable in soups and gumbos.

Okra grows on a wide range of soil types and tolerates large variations in soil reaction (pH). Good drainage is essential. This does not mean just surface runoff, but that water will percolate through the soil.

Any good garden soil should be satisfactory, although a sandy loam soil with a porous clay subsoil is ideal. Adding manure or organic matter in some other form is usually helpful. Also, it is generally a good idea to apply a complete fertilizer, relatively high in phosphorus, before planting the seed.

From 1 to 1.5 pounds of 6-12-6 fertilizer per 25 feet of row may be used in a garden, or a similar amount of nutrients provided by another grade and rate. It should be worked in to a depth of about 4 inches.

As okra has a long growing season, application of additional readily available nitrogen during the season is often beneficial, especially on lighter soil types. If this is done, 2 moderate applications of nitrogen fertilizer 4 to 6 weeks apart would be preferable to 1 heavy application.

When fertilizing okra, give care to the rate and timing of nitrogen applications. This is because of the plant's tendency to become excessively vegetative and produce few pods if excessive nitrogen is available. Excess nitrogen can result from either applying too much fertilizer or breakdown of soil organic matter during the growing season.

Include only light to moderate rates of nitrogen in the preplanting fertilizer, especially on soil relatively high

W. D. Kimbrough is Professor Emeritus, and L. G. Jones and J. F. Fontenot are Professors in the Department of Horticulture, Louisiana State University, Baton Rouge.

Allan Stoner

in organic matter. Withhold the first side-dressing of nitrogen until after a few pods have set on each plant. Then you may make a moderate application of nitrogen fertilizer (⅛ to ¼ pound of ammonium nitrate or equivalent per 25 feet of row, depending on organic matter content of the soil). At this time, the plants usually will be about knee-high, depending on the variety.

As the season progresses and the plants reach a height of waist to shoulder, they may require a second moderate application of nitrogen fertilizer as side-dressing, especially if you intend to harvest pods late in the season.

Important Varieties

Okra varieties differ considerably in size of plants and shape of pods. Height of plant will vary from 5 to 10 feet after a few months of growth. Length of the internodes and the degree of lateral branching—both of which are influenced by the plant's genetic makeup—as well as growing conditions determine size of the plant. Dwarf varieties have shorter internodes.

Pod shape ranges from short to long and from nearly round to very ridged. Pod diameter also varies.

Okra varieties and strains differ greatly in plant growth, pod pigmentation, leaves, and stems. They also vary in leaf shape and flowers. Thus, okra may be enjoyed by the homeowner for ornamental purposes as well as for food.

Seed catalogs usually list about six varieties. A short description of the most important varieties follows:

Clemson Spineless is of medium plant height, about 5 feet; mature pods are 5 to 6 inches long, moderately ridged, straight, and green. The pods are very smooth and have few spines. The first fruit for harvest matures in about 55 days. It can be used fresh or processed.

Emerald is also of medium height, about 5 feet, with mature pods 8 inches long. The pods are straight, round, smooth, very slender and deep green. Production starts some 50 days from planting, and pods can be used fresh or processed.

Louisiana Green Velvet is medium-tall, 7 to 9 feet, with mature pods about 7 inches long, slender, round, straight, and green. Production starts about 60 days after planting. Pods can be used fresh or processed.

Perkins Mammoth Long Pod is very tall, 10 to 12 feet; mature pods are 7 to 8 inches long, ridged and green. The first fruit for harvest matures in about 60 days. It can be used fresh or processed.

Gold Coast is of medium plant height, about 4½ feet; mature pods are short and round, green, straight, and about 3 to 4 inches long. The first fruit is ready for harvest in some 55 days. It has a long shelf life, and is recommended for fresh use only.

Size of the garden plot may determine the variety to plant. Smaller growing plants may be preferable in gardens that aren't very big.

As okra is a warm weather vegetable, don't plant it until the soil

Okra plants showing hibiscus-type flower and young tender pods.

warms up in spring. If early okra is desired, place black plastic on the rows prepared for planting. Or grow plants in peat pots and transplant them to the garden when the soil is warm enough.

Soak Seed Overnight

Getting a good stand of okra is not as easy as with many other vegetables. Soaking seed overnight in water before planting usually results in quicker germination and a better plant stand. Seed generally is planted in the prepared row, or 3 or 4 seeds may be planted in hills at desired spacings. Plant seed at a depth of ½ to 1 inch, depending on soil type. The deeper planting is for sandier soils. Rows should be 3 to 5 feet apart.

After the seed germinates, thin the plants to a spacing of 1 to 2 feet, depending on the variety. Plant okra where it will get full sunlight.

Weeds and grass should be controlled. Since drought severe enough to affect the growth of okra plants occurs commonly in the South, irrigation may be needed. Too much water may cause excessive vegetative growth of plants and less pod production.

The okra plant and pods may have small spines which some people are allergic to. Plant breeders have developed varieties with fewer spines, especially on the pods. At harvest time wear gloves and a long sleeved shirt or blouse as skin protection. With large plants and hot weather, harvesting okra can be mighty uncomfortable.

Harvest Carefully

Cut the pods with a knife or shears. In any case, harvest very carefully so as not to injure the pods or the plant. Harvest pods when they are large enough to give a good yield but before they become fibrous. This is usually when the pods are about four inches long or between the fourth and seventh day from the time the bloom opens, depending on variety and weather conditions. Perference of the harvester as regards pod size is also a consideration.

The okra pod becomes fibrous from the tip down. To be edible a pod should allow a knife blade to pass through it without providing noticeable resistance. Okra pods that get fibrous or tough on the plant will slow down the plant's growth and decrease yield.

Periods between harvests should be short, usually not over two or three days. Even then there will be considerable variation in the length of pods harvested.

The harvested pods should be handled with care, as they bruise easily. The pods will wilt rather quickly when harvested during warm periods. Therefore they should be used or stored at 45° to 50° F and relatively high humidity as soon as possible after harvest. A home refrigerator provides adequate storage conditions.

Cutting Back

Sometimes when plants get too large they are cut back and allowed to sprout again near the soil surface. If this is done, apply a top-dressing of a readily available nitrogenous fertilizer.

A 25-foot row of okra should produce 25 to 75 pounds of edible pods, depending on variety, care, weather conditions, and length of harvest season.

You can grow your own seed if you raise only one variety of okra and have no near neighbor growing another variety. Late in the season allow a few plants to develop mature seed. After removing seed from the pod, dry thoroughly and store it in the refrigerator in a closed container until the next spring. Then you can be assured of having seed of the kind wanted at planting time.

Several pests can injure okra, with

nematodes probably the most serious. Gardens that have remained in the same location for several years usually are infested with these small round worms. The only remedy is to periodically treat the soil with materials that will kill most of them. Obtain directions for treating soil from your county agent.

With other conditions favorable, a fair crop of okra may be produced despite nematodes. But the harvest season is likely to be shortened.

Wilts may kill or injure okra plants. The organisms that cause wilt are soil-borne and require soil treatment.

Several insects also may cause damage to okra. These include the corn earworm, which eats into the pod, and stinkbugs and ants which are especially troublesome late in the season.

Recommendations for controlling pests vary as new products become available or old ones are taken off the market. Consult your county agent for current recommendations.

Stink bug, which damages okra, produces foul odor when annoyed.

Miscellany, Including Celeriac, Horseradish, Artichoke, Peanuts, Vegetable Soybeans

by Homer N. Metcalf and Milo Burnham

Plants discussed in this chapter will provide both experienced and beginning gardeners with an introduction to the fascination of growing uncommon vegetables. Once culture of the easier vegetables has been mastered, the natural tendency of gardeners is to extend their experience. Unusual vegetables which may require special production techniques provide a stimulating challenge.

Information is provided for celeriac, chayote, dasheen, globe antichoke, horseradish, husk tomato, martynia, mushrooms, peanuts, sunchoke, vegetable soybeans, and watercress. Of these, celeriac, chayote, husk tomato, martynia, peanuts and sunchoke occur naturally in some parts of the Western Hemisphere. The others are from Eurasia or Oceania. Irrespective of their ultimate origins, they all are fascinating to grow and delightful to eat.

Because these vegetables are, for the most part, of no or minor commercial importance in the United States, comparatively little research has been devoted to them. Hence, the cultural practices suggested are often less exact than would be the case for major vegetables. Experience will certainly improve the home gardener's skill in growing them, but lack of experience should not deter him from giving them a whirl.

Since soil conditions vary so widely over the country, no specific recommendations for fertilizer usage are included, other than for fresh manure. In general, most efficient utilization of applied fertilizers will be obtained where 5% to 6% soil organic matter can be maintained. Home gardeners are urged to follow locally applicable fertilizer recommendations based on the results of soil tests that can be obtained through their county Extension office or commercial soil testing laboratories.

Resistant varieties are the first line of defense against diseases, insects, nematodes and other troubles. Where resistant varieties are not available, the home gardener should consult his county Extension office for information about recommended pesticides.

Celeriac

Celeriac (*Apium graveolens* L. var. *rapaceum* DC.) is a botanical variety of celery, differing from that vegetable in producing at the base of the plant a large, turnip-like swelling that may be as much as 4 inches in diameter. This rather bulbous base is the commonly eaten part of the plant.

Celeriac—like celery, carrots, parsley, parsnips and dill—is a member of the Parsley Family (Umbelliferae or Apiaceae). The plant is a biennial, growing to about 36 inches in height, but in gardens it is treated as an annual. It is naturally distributed in marsh areas in the temperate zones of South America, South Africa, New Zealand and Eurasia.

Celeriac "bulbs" may be boiled like potatoes, and put to all the uses made of boiled potatoes. Boiling time for celeriac will be somewhat longer than for potatoes. Celeriac may also be grated raw as a salad topping. An intriguing use is serving sliced, boiled celeriac with French dressing as an hors d'oeuvre. Celeriac has the odor typical of celery due to the presence of a volatile oil. Celeriac is comparatively low in nutrients.

Homer N. Metcalf is Professor of Horticulture, Montana State University, Bozeman. Milo Burnham is Extension Horticulturist, Mississippi State University, Mississippi State.

Although several varieties of celeriac are grown in Europe, Giant Prague has been the only one readily available in the United States. A newer variety is Alabaster.

The culture of celeriac is very similar to that for its close relative, celery. It is a long-season vegetable, requiring nearly 6 months from seeding to harvest, and growing best where the monthly growing season mean temperature is 60° to 65° F (approximately 15.5° to 18.5° C). It is unlikely to be grown successfully in areas or at seasons where monthly mean growing season temperatures exceed 70° to 75° F or are lower than 45°. Since celeriac plants grow rather slowly, a freeze-free growing season of at least 110 days is desirable.

The home gardener has two options for production of celeriac. He may either purchase seedlings from a vegetable plant grower or raise them himself. The use of purchased transplants is suggested for short growing season areas, while gardeners living in milder climates may take either route. Gardeners raising their own transplants should be aware that celeriac must have 60° to 65° F night temperatures throughout the seedling and early transplant stages if premature seed-stalk development is to be avoided.

When home-grown transplants are to be used, the gardener will soon discover that celeriac seeds are quite small (approximately 70,000 per ounce). They will remain viable for 4 to 5 years under cool, dry storage conditions. Thus, one need purchase only a small quantity of seed at a time.

Seeds may be sown in flats or individual peat pots. If sown in flats, a seeding rate of 8 seeds per inch of row is suggested. If seeded in individual peat pots, about 10 seeds per pot should be sown, with the extra seedlings later thinned to one per pot. Celeriac seeds characteristically have germination percentages of 50% to 70%, and germinate best at a 70° F minimum temperature. If maintained at this temperature, germination should be complete in about 10 days. Following germination, night temperatures of 60° to 65° are desirable, with daytime temperatures 10° warmer. If seeded directly in the garden, germination and emergence will be materially slower.

Flat-grown seedlings should be transplanted to individual pots as soon as the first true leaves develop. Weekly feedings with a complete liquid fertilizer will promote sturdy growth.

Plants will be ready to transplant to the garden 8 to 12 weeks after seed-sowing, or when they are 3 to 4 inches tall.

Celeriac needs a deep, fertile, well-manured soil which retains moisture well throughout the growing season. Fresh manure, if available, should be applied at the rate of 55 to 92 pounds per hundred square feet. The quantities of lime and commercial fertilizers used should be governed by the results of soil tests. Since celeriac is a gross feeder, two or more side-dressings with readily soluble nitrogenous fertilizers during the growing season are suggested. Regular irrigation will prove beneficial.

As a rule, wait until 5 days after the average last spring freeze-date to set out the transplants, at which time maples may be coming into leaf in many areas. In the garden, the transplants may be spaced, or seedlings thinned, to stand 6 to 7 inches apart in rows 24 to 36 inches apart. An alternative is to check-row the plants at 15 to 18 inches apart in rows 18 inches apart, a system more likely to produce exhibition-quality plants.

Higher quality celeriac will be produced if sideshoots and withered leaves are removed as they appear. Mulching the rows with lawngrass clippings is sometimes practiced, especially where no manure has been used and irrigation is not available. A further quality-producing practice is to draw soil up around the plants to the level of the leaves about two weeks before harvest. This will yield a whiter product, and is called "blanching".

Celeriac will generally be ready to harvest in October, or when the "bulbs" have attained diameters of 2 to 2.5 inches. The plants may be pulled or dug, depending on soil conditions. Tops are trimmed off and any branching basal roots removed. Yields of 200 bulbs per 100 feet of row are a reasonable expectation. The trimmed "bulbs" can be stored in moist sand in a cool root cellar, in a vegetable pit, or in colored plastic sacks in a refrigerator. Properly stored, they will keep about 6 months.

Celeriac troubles will be similar to those afflicting celery.

Chayote

Chayote (*Sechium edule* Swartz) is popularly known as mirliton and vegetable pear in South Louisiana where it is grown and relished. In the mild-winter regions along the Gulf Coast and in parts of California, chayote is grown for its light-green, pear-shaped fruits that are served with salad dressing or stuffed after boiling with ground meat or seafood.

The fruit is considered an excellent substitute for summer squash, but is of little nutritional value. Historically chayote dates back to the Aztecs before the Spanish conquest.

Chayote is related to all the cucumbers, pumpkins, squash, melons and gourds so popular with gardeners, but differs from them in having only one large seed. In Central America the plant is grown as a perennial and the large tuberous roots that develop over a 2- to 3-year period are eaten after roasting, boiling or frying and they are sometimes candied in sugar. The roots contain about 70 percent water and 20 percent starch. The young

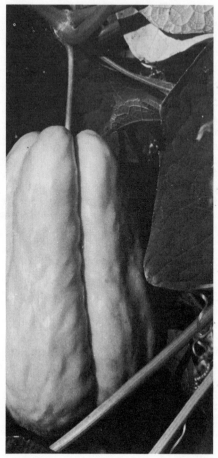

Milo Burnham

shoots are also sometimes cooked as a green vegetable.

In the southern United States, chayote is mostly grown as an annual since freezing kills the entire plant. Heavy mulching may protect the roots from freezing, and the plant will resprout in spring. In Northern States the short growing season will more than likely prevent fruiting since the plant is day-length sensitive and flowers only in late summer and early fall.

Chayote hanging on vine has pear shape and deeply furrowed surface.

Seed of chayote is difficult to locate since the whole fruit is used as a seed. It is not marketed through retail seed catalogs, and is often available only in localities where the plant is grown.

When all danger of frost and cold weather has passed in spring and the soil is warm, plant the whole fruit on a slant with the broad end down and the stem end slightly exposed. If the seed has sprouted before planting, which is often the case, cut the sprout back to a length of about 2 inches.

The vine grows rapidly when planted in a rich, well-drained soil with plenty of organic matter. Since the vine is large and vigorous, plant the seeds no closer than 10 feet apart and provide a trellis or some means of support. One plant may be sufficient for any garden since each vine produces 30 to 35 fruits. The plant should be supplied with generous amounts of water, and fertilizer rich in potash but low in nitrogen. An oversupply of nitrogen will result in excessive growth at the expense of fruit production.

Chayote is monoecious (male and female flower parts in separate flowers but on the same plant) and is dependent on flower-visiting insects for pollination. Bees swarm to the flowers for nectar. The fruits require about 30 days from pollination to mature sufficiently to harvest, and may weigh up to 2 pounds.

The type most commonly grown in the southern United States produces light-green, pear-shaped fruit.

Insect and disease problems of chayote are the same as for pumpkins, squash and other relatives. Among the insect pests are striped and spotted cucumber beetles, squash bug, squash vine borer and pickle worm. Disease problems include powdery and downy mildews.

To save seed, allow the fruits to reach full maturity on the vine but harvest them before they sprout. Wrap each fruit separately and store it in a cool ventilated place.

Dasheen

Dasheen (*Colocasia esculenta* Schott), also known as oriental taro, is a large perennial plant cultivated for its underground corms and tubers. In the United States its cultivation is limited to warm coastal regions. Closely related to ornamental elephant's ear, caladium, calla and the native jack-in-the-pulpit, dasheen differs from them in producing edible corms and tubers that contain practically no calcium oxalate, a harmful chemical. Dasheen varieties also differ from most taros in this respect.

Taro was first introduced into the southern United States with shipments of African slaves who used it for food. The origin of taro has been traced to India and following its dispersal it has served as a staple food crop of Pacific Island dwellers for thousands of years. In the early 1900's a superior type of oriental taro traced to China and known as dasheen was introduced into the United States. This type largely replaced the earlier introduced, acrid, coarse African types.

At one time dasheen was considered as a possible substitute crop on lands too wet to grow Irish potatoes. Nutritional properties of the tubers are similar to potatoes. The tubers can be prepared in any way that potatoes can and the flavor is described as delicate and nutty.

Dasheen requires a frost-free growing period of about seven months. It is therefore limited to the lowland Coastal Plains from South Carolina to Texas. In Hawaii, dasheen is a very common garden plant, used to make the popular poi.

Production of tubers is greatest in rich, loamy, well-drained soils with an abundance of moisture. Clay soils produce low quality dasheen, as do long droughts followed by regrowth and prolonged wet periods.

Plant whole tubers weighing 2 to 5 ounces, 2 to 3 inches deep, at 2-foot intervals in rows about 4 feet apart.

Begin planting about April 1 or earlier, up to 2 weeks before the average date of the last killing frost in spring. It is also possible to start plants indoors and set them in the garden when frost danger is past.

With adequate moisture and fertilizer the plants will reach 4 to 5 feet in height. Apply a preplant application of fertilizer and an equal amount before the plants reach 2 feet in height.

Dasheen is shallow rooted so a heavy mulch will help prevent loss of soil moisture in dry periods.

The corms and cormels (tubers) are mature enough to harvest when the tops have completely died down in fall (October-November). Dig the plants in dry weather if at all possible to avoid injury to the corms. The crop may be stored in the ground and dug as needed where the soil is well drained.

Each plant when dug should have at least one large central corm surrounded by smaller tubers with a combined weight of 2½ to 8 pounds.

The tubers are reported to be of better eating quality and will store longer than the large corm. Tubers will keep for several months at 50° F when they are provided with good air circulation.

Young unrolling leaves can be eaten as a table green. They are a rich source of vitamins A and C and when properly prepared are free of the harmful calcium oxalate. Leaves should be boiled with a large pinch of baking soda for 15 minutes and then boiled in fresh water till tender. The stored corms and tubers can be forced to sprout in the dark and the blanched shoots prepared and eaten.

A major disease of dasheen is root-knot nematodes. Plant only tubers free of evidence of nematodes. Storage rots occur if the tubers are dug before they are fully mature or if proper temperature and adequate ventilation are not provided in storage.

Magnifico globe artichoke with large terminal buds.

Globe Artichoke

Globe artichoke (*Cynara scolymus* L.) plants look like large thistles and may reach 3 to 4 feet in height and cover several square feet with their large, prickly deep-cut leaves. Artichokes are not for the gardener with limited space. Climate requirements restrict their culture even more.

Globe artichokes grow best in frost-free areas with cool, foggy summers. No wonder their commercial production in the United States is limited to one small area in coastal California! However, home gardeners with less than ideal growing conditions can successfully produce artichokes. A variety known as Creole grows in southern Louisiana, and a few artichokes have been grown in Michigan. The most familiar artichoke—and

Vincent E. Rubatzky

232

available in the seed trade—is Green Globe.

Historically, artichokes originated in southern Europe where they were cultivated since Roman times. They were brought to California by Spanish explorers. Artichokes are grown for the soft fleshy receptacle and thickened bases of the bracts of the flower heads. Each plant produces several stalks and each stalk bears several flower heads.

The plant is an herbaceous perennial that grows best in a rich, well-drained soil supplied with plenty of organic matter and having a pH of about 6.0. It lives for several years and increases in production provided it doesn't freeze

Seed of the Green Globe variety is advertised in several home garden seed and plant catalogs, but germination is apt to be low and the plants produced quite variable to type. Seed germination is improved by storing it for 2 weeks in the refrigerator in moist peat moss. Plant the seeds in individual cups or pots 4 to 6 weeks before you want to set the plants out. This will give you an early start and avoid the shock of transplanting.

Globe artichokes are best propagated by crown divisions or rooted suckers or sprouts from the base of the plant. Space the plants 4 to 6 feet apart and supply them with adequate fertilizer and water during the growing season. The plants grow best at temperatures from the mid-60's to the mid-70's (degrees Fahrenheit). At higher temperatures the buds open rapidly and the bracts become fibrous and tough.

Stalks and buds appear in late summer or early fall. In frost-free areas, flower bud production continues through winter into early spring. Cut artichokes while the buds are still tight. In overmature artichokes the green bracts loosen and point out and purple flowers show. The Creole variety is an exception since its bud bracts naturally point out. As each stalk is finished, remove it completely from the plant.

In northern gardens, most attempts to produce globe artichokes are unsuccessful. Frost and freezing temperatures kill the plants, and heavy mulches used for protection often result in the crowns rotting. In many instances the plants freeze before becoming large enough to flower.

Horseradish

Horseradish (*Armoracia rusticana* Gaertn., B. Mey. & Scherb.) is a member of the Mustard Family (Cruciferae or Brassicaceae). It is believed to be native in southeastern Europe, but is grown in cool temperate climates over much of the world and has frequently escaped from cultivation. The "radish" part of the common name derives from the latin, *radix,* for root, while the "horse" part may allude to the strong flavor of the root, or to the plant's coarse texture.

Although condiments derived from roots of the horseradish are now quite familiar, primary use of the plant before the 16th Century was for its alleged medicinal properties. However, both leaves and roots were eaten in Germany during medieval times. Today, peeled roots are either grated and prepared with diluted vinegar, or boiled, pureed, and used in preparing various sauces. The pungent flavor is due to the presence of the glucoside sinigrin.

Horseradish is a hardy perennial that produces a whorl of large, coarse-textured leaves. The seeds mature but rarely, and are not used in propagating the crop, which is raised from root cuttings.

A deep, rich, moist loamy soil is best for horseradish. It has also been grown successfully on organic soils. On hard, shallow, stony soils the roots tend to be malformed and yields are reduced. Unless the soil is already fertile and in good tilth, it should be manured the autumn prior to planting at the rate of 55 to 92 pounds of fresh manure per hundred square feet, and plowed or spaded to a depth of at least 10 inches. Where no manure is available, grow soil-improving crops for plowing down in the the autumn of the year preceding that in which the crop will be planted. In mild climates, a winter-grown soil-improving crop may be spring-plowed.

Phosphate and potash mineral fertilizers should be roto-tilled or spaded into the soil before planting. Manure should not be spring-applied in the year of planting, but nitrogenous fertilizers may be applied broadcast and the ground reworked at that season. Amounts of commercial fertilizers to be used should be guided by the results of soil tests.

Horseradish is best grown from root cuttings, sometimes called "sets". Sets are small or slender roots, 8 to 14 inches long, that are trimmed from the main roots at autumn harvest. As these cuttings are removed from the main root, it is wise to make a square cut at the top and a slanting cut at the bottom as an aid to subsequent proper planting procedure. The sets are cleaned, bundled, packaged and held under refrigeration or in a vegetable pit or root cellar until planting time the following spring.

An alternative procedure is to leave a few plants in the garden over winter for spring digging and taking of cuttings at or near planting time.

In spring, the fall-plowed soil should be well worked, including incorporation of any spring-applied mineral fertilizers, especially nitrogenous ones. It is a good idea to let the worked-up soil settle a few days before planting.

Horseradish is commonly grown in rows spaced 30 inches apart, with the plants spaced 24 inches apart in the rows. Yield estimates vary from 15 to 35 pounds of roots per 50 feet of row. Size of the horseradish plot will depend on the popularity of horseradish preparations with the family, but one or two dozen plants should be enough for the average family.

In planting, make furrows 3 to 5 inches deep. Plant the cuttings with the tops all in one direction in the row, dropping a cutting every 24 inches. As the cutting is dropped, draw a little soil over the lower end with your foot and tamp firmly. After all cuttings are dropped, they are covered with soil to slightly above ground level (to allow for soil settling), being sure that the soil is firmly in contact with the cutting.

Cultivation for weed control in horseradish (and other garden crops) is especially important early in the season when the plants are relatively small. If mechanical cultivation is practiced, it is best to cultivate in the same direction that the cuttings were dropped—toward the top end.

To grow high quality horseradish, remove all top and side roots, leaving only those at the bottom of the set. This is done twice during the growing season, first when the largest leaves are 8 to 10 inches long, and again about 6 weeks later.

To remove top and side roots from the sets, first carefully remove the soil around the top end of the main root, leaving roots at the lower end of the set undisturbed. Raise the crown and remove all but the best sprout or crown of leaves. Rub off any small roots that have started from the top or sides of the set, leaving only those at the bottom. Return the set to its original position and replace the soil. This procedure is called lifting and produces a relatively smooth root, free from side roots.

Horseradish makes its greatest growth during late summer and early autumn. For this reason, harvest usually is delayed until October or early November, or just before the ground freezes. In digging, it may prove wise to dig a trench 12 to 24 inches deep along one side of the row. Then, working from the opposite side of the row with a shovel or spading fork, dig the roots, using the tops as a handle for pulling laterally from the loosened soil. The tops should be trimmed from the roots to within one inch of the crown. Side and bottom roots are trimmed off, reserving the laterals for the succeeding season's crop.

If you wish to store horseradish roots for frequent fresh grinding, they may be cleaned, washed, and stored in plastic wrapping in a refrigerator, vegetable pit or root cellar. When stored in the refrigerator, protect horseradish roots from light to prevent their turning green. For this purpose, recycle the colored plastic bags in which potatoes often are marketed.

In relatively mild climates where frost penetration of the soil is not extensive, the roots may be stored in an 8- to 10-inch deep trench lined with clean straw. Place roots on the straw and cover with a 6-inch layer of clean straw. As the weather becomes colder, cover the straw with 6 inches or more of soil before the ground freezes. This will protect the roots from freezing injury.

Occasionally, horseradish may suffer from attacks of root rot. To avoid this, select only disease-free root cuttings for planting stock, and rotate the planting site so that horseradish is not grown on the same piece of ground more often than every 3 to 4 years.

Leafhoppers, flea beetles and grasshoppers may attack horseradish foliage. Leafhoppers spread the virus disease known in the inland Northwest as "curly top", which can have devastating effects on this and many other vegetables. There is no cure. Apply approved insecticides as soon as the insects appear. Consult your county Extension agent for current information on pesticides.

The most common way of preparing horseradish for table use is by peeling or scraping the roots and removing all defects. Then, grate the root directly into white wine vinegar or distilled vinegar. Avoid using cider vinegar, as it causes discoloration in the grated horseradish within a rather short time.

Depending on your preference, the vinegar may be slightly diluted before use. Bottle the horseradish and cap the containers as soon as possible after grating. Refrigerate the prepared product at all times to preserve the pungent flavor. It will keep for a few weeks. Then prepare a fresh supply.

Horseradish may also be dried, ground to a powder and put up in bottles in a dry form. So prepared, horseradish will keep much longer than the freshly grated product, but is not generally as high quality.

Husk Tomato

Husk tomato or ground cherry (*Physalis* spp.) is a member of the Nightshade Family (Solanaceae). The generic name is from the Greek for a bladder, in allusion to the charactistically inflated calyx ("husk"). Most *Physalis* species occur naturally in the Western Hemisphere. The forms of husk tomatoes in cultivation are usually ascribed to *Physalis pruinosa* L or *P. pubescens* L., but these species may be confused in gardens, and other species also may be involved.

Husk tomato plants are annuals growing 18 to 40 inches in height. They often inhabit sandy soils in nature. The fruit, which is the edible portion of the plant, is a berry completely enclosed in the thin, inflated calyx or husk.

The fruit may be eaten fresh-ripe, or prepared in a number of ways, including fried, baked, stewed, in meat dishes, soups or salads, or as dessert sauces and preserves. It is a common ingredient in Latin American cuisine.

Seeds are infrequently listed in

catalogs. An improved form, developed from Guatemalan material by the Iowa Agricultural Experiment Station, was introduced some years ago.

Plant growing and general culture are much the same as for the tomato. In cool climates, starting the plants indoors or in a greenhouse and transplanting 6-week-old seedlings to the garden about 5 days after the average date of the last spring freeze should help in attaining a good crop. Like tomatoes, husk tomatoes will respond to favorable levels of soil fertility and ample irrigation.

The fruits begin to mature from mid-summer to late summer, turning from green to yellow and becoming somewhat soft during ripening. They are not adapted for long-term storage and should be used or processed shortly after harvest. Yields as much as 2.5 pounds per plant have been achieved. Ten plants should produce enough husk tomatoes to supply the average family.

Troubles will be similar to those afflicting tomatoes.

Martynia

Martynia (Proboscidea louisianica [Miller] Thellung) is native to the Southwest but gardeners throughout the Nation who are interested in unusual plants grow it. The dried seed pod has an unusual appearance which accounts for the popular name "Unicorn Plant" and for the fact that several retail seed and plant catalogs offer seed. Dried pods are used in floral arrangements and as novelty items. Young immature seed pods can be pickled sweet like cucumbers.

Plant the seed ½ inch deep at 18- to 24-inch intervals in rows 3 feet apart. In Northern States start the plants indoors and set them out in the garden after frost danger is past. The plants grow about 18 inches tall and have a spread of some 30 inches. General cultural requirements are about the same as for okra.

Mushrooms

Edible mushrooms (Agaricus bisporus) are not easily produced in the home because of the exacting conditions required. Even so, mushroom spawn and culture kits are offered for sale by several retail plant and seed suppliers. However, a recently described method for small scale cultivation of mushrooms used for demonstration and class study provides a more certain way for the serious home gardener to grow mushrooms.

The reference to the article describing the method is: San Antonio, James P. 1975. "Commercial and small scale cultivation of the mushroom, Agaricus bisporus (Lange) Sing." HortScience. Vol. 10(5):451—458. Your library may have the article, or you can obtain a copy from the Vegetable Laboratory, Agricultural Research Center, Beltsville, Md. 20705.

Peanuts

Peanuts (Arachis hypogaea L.), a popular home garden crop in the Southeast and Southwest, are unique among garden plants. Showy yellow flowers are borne above ground but the ripened ovary and seeds (peanuts) develop below the ground.

The peanut originated in South America, was carried to Africa and Europe by Old World navigators and explorers, and was shipped to America as on-board food for slaves. Peanuts are now grown along the East Coast from Virginia to Florida, and along the Gulf Coast to Texas and in all adjoining inland States. Gardeners hold the peanut with the same high regard as Southern peas, okra and butter beans.

"Chock full" describes the nutritional and energy value of peanuts. They can be eaten raw, boiled, steamed or roasted. Raw, cured peanuts are rich in vegetable protein and oil and contain 564 calories per 100 grams.

Peanuts are divided into four general categories: Virginia, Runner, Spanish and Valencia. Virginia and Runner types are large-seeded and contain 2 seeds per pod. Spanish and Valencia are small-seeded with the Spanish having 2 to 3 seeds and the Valencia 3 to 6 seeds per pod.

Peanuts require a long, warm growing season (110 to 120 days). They flower 6 to 8 weeks after planting. Following self-pollination and wilting of the flower, the ovary (peg) emerges and grows downward until it enters the soil and the nut begins to form.

Best soils for peanuts are coarse textured (sandy loams) adequately supplied with calcium and with a pH of 5.8 to 6.2. Add lime to soils with a pH below 5.8. Spanish types grow in both fine and coarse textured soils, but the Virginia types should be limited to coarse soils.

Plant Spanish types with a spacing of 4 to 6 inches in rows 24 inches apart. Virginia types need more room so plant them 6 to 8 inches apart in rows 36 inches apart. Plant only shelled seed. One-half pound of seed will plant 100 feet of row. Plant the seed 1½ to 2 inches deep in coarse soils but only 1 inch deep in fine soils. Planting can begin about 2 weeks after the average date of the last killing frost in spring.

Prepare the garden soil completely before planting. All crop residues should be turned under in fall to permit decomposition. Do not plant peanuts in the same location 2 years in a row, to prevent build-up of diseases.

A soil test is the best means of determining fertilizer needs. Where the garden has been heavily fertilized for previous crops, you may not need to apply additional fertilizer since peanuts are good foragers. The young peanut plant is sensitive to fertilizer burn, so spread any fertilizer applied over the entire planting area rather than putting it in the row.

A shortage of water when the plants are flowering vigorously and when the pegs are entering the soil will reduce the yield of peanuts. As harvest draws near, do not water peanuts. Any excess water at this time may break dormancy and cause the mature peanuts to sprout.

To prevent development of "pops" (empty pods) the soil must have a good supply of available calcium. On soils known to be low in calcium, sprinkle about 2½ pounds of gypsum per 100 feet of row over the plants when they begin to bloom.

Cultivate the soil to control weeds and to keep the soil loose so the pegs can penetrate the surface. Once the pods are developing in the soil, cultivation without damaging the plants is almost impossible. Do not throw or pull soil to the plants while cultivating. Peanut plants are low growing; covering branches and leaves with soil kills leaves and interferes with flowering.

As peanuts mature the leaves will begin to turn yellow. Since flowers appear for several weeks, all the peanuts do not mature at the same time. If you delay harvest until the last formed pods are mature, the first-formed pods may rot or sprout or be left in the ground when the plants are dug.

Dig the entire plant and turn it over in the row with the peanuts facing up. Pull peanuts for boiling at digging time when they contain 40 to 50 percent water (the peanut inside of the shell will rattle). After several days under good drying conditions, moisture content of the exposed pods drops to about 15 percent and the plants can be moved to a warm, airy place and stacked for 2 to 3 weeks to complete curing before the peanuts are stripped from the plants. Some gardeners stack the plants around poles out in the open until the peanuts are cured.

Several insects and diseases attack

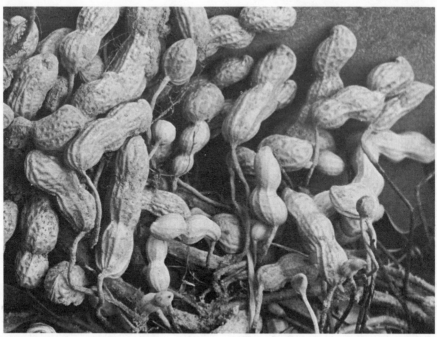

peanuts and reduce yields or kill the plants. Corn earworm, cutworms, fall armyworms and velvetbean caterpillars feed on the foliage while the whitefringed beetle feeds on underground plant parts. Leafspots and southern stem blight are among the most serious diseases.

Leaves infected with leafspots drop from the plants and result in "false" maturity and low yields and poor quality. Leafspot diseases can be controlled by spraying with recommended fungicides and changing the location of peanuts in the garden every year.

Southern stem blight (stem rot) attacks stems, roots, pods and pod stems. This disease is best controlled by turning under plant residues in fall so they have time to decompose, and by moving the location of peanuts in the garden every year.

Sunchoke (Jerusalem Artichoke)

The frequently used common name,

Jerusalem artichoke, for *Helianthus tuberosus* L. is really a misnomer, and the plant might better be known as sunchoke. The plant has no biological association with Biblical lands, being native in North America east of the 20-inch precipitation line, ranging from Kansas and Minnesota east and north to Nova Scotia.

The "Jerusalem" part of the common name is thought to be a corruption of "girasole", the Italian name for the sunflower (*Helianthus annuus* L.), to which the sunchoke is closely related. The literal meaning of "girasole" is "turning to the sun". Further, the sunchoke is not really an artichoke, since that common name should be reserved for *Cynara scolymus* L., the globe artichoke. All these plants are members of the Composite Family (Compositae or Asteraceae).

Mature and immature peanut pods, showing fruiting habit of the plant.

Early adventurers and colonists found the sunchoke being used as a food crop by Amerinds along the Atlantic coast. It was taken to Europe early in the 17th Century. The sunchoke is now cultivated and naturalized extensively on well-drained soils throughout the cool-temperature climatic regions of the world.

Sunchokes are grown for the edible tubers produced on the ends and branches of underground stems. The tubers may reach 4 inches in length and 2 to 2.75 inches in diameter. They are of special interest because the principal storage carbohydrate in them is inulin, a substance reputed to be of value in the diet of diabetics as a substitute for ordinary starch. Sunchoke tubers may be prepared for the table in the same ways that potatoes are used.

The sunchoke plant is a rather coarse, rough-surfaced perennial that grows 6 to 9 feet tall. The leaves are large, 4 to 8 inches long, oblong and toothed. At the base of the plant they may appear to be opposite each other, but in the upper part of the plant they

Thin-skinned, often knobby subterranean stem tubers are edible portions of sunchoke plant (Jerusalem artichoke).

may be alternate. The flowering heads terminate the branched stems, looking much like small sunflowers, with yellow ray and disk florets.

In choosing a site for sunchokes in the garden, keep in mind their potential height and vigor. Although sunchokes will grow on soils too dry or infertile for potatoes or beets, they will respond readily to better growing conditions. If they can be planted on sandy or loamy soils, the task of digging the tubers will be much easier. It is wise to plant them where they will be more or less out of the way and not shade other sun-loving plants.

Sunchokes are sensitive to borate herbicides, so areas that have been treated with them should be avoided.

Cultural practices for sunchoke are generally similar to those for the potato. Although sunchoke is a perennial plant, it is usually treated as an

D. H. Fritts

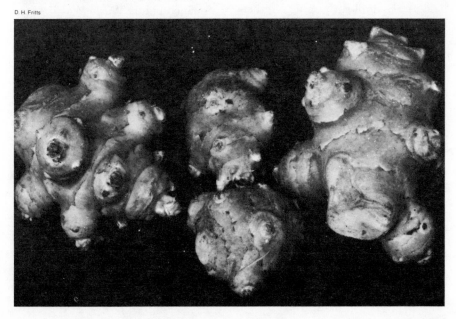

annual in the garden. Planting may be done either in autumn at harvest time, or in spring as soon as the soil can be worked readily. Both white- and red-skinned forms are known, but the red is quite rare.

For planting stock, either whole tubers or tuber-pieces of about 2-ounce weight are suggested. These should be planted about 4 inches deep and spaced about 24 inches apart in the row, the rows being spaced 36 to 40 inches apart. If the soil is very fertile, spacing may be increased.

Very little information about fertilizer requirements for sunchokes is available, but European experiments suggest the potash requirement may be high. Hence it is probable that fertilizer and irrigation regimes producing good yields of potatoes will give favorable results with sunchokes. Established plants require relatively little care beyond weed control. The average gardeners may expect to harvest about 3 bushels of tubers per 100 feet of row.

Since sunchoke tubers are hardy, harvest may be delayed until the tops have frozen down in autumn or even be deferred until early spring. Spring-dug tubers will taste somewhat sweeter than autumn-dug ones.

Digging will be easier if the tops are first removed. Using a spading fork or potato hook, a thorough search for tubers should be undertaken, extending some distance from the plant. Missed tubers can lead to a weedy growth of sunchokes the succeeding year.

Because sunchoke tubers are thin-skinned and do not store nearly as well as potato tubers, dig them only as needed so long as the soil remains workable in autumn. When freeze-up is at hand, enough tubers to supply winter needs should be dug, cleaned, washed, and prepared for storage.

Sunchoke tubers store best at 32° F and 90% to 95% relative humidity. If these conditions can be provided, tubers may be stored successfully up to 5 months. It should be possible to store an adequate supply in damp sand in a root cellar or vegetable pit, or in colored plastic bags in a refrigerator.

Sunchokes are seldom bothered by insects or diseases.

Vegetable Soybeans

Soybeans are members of the genus *Glycine* L., which consists of 10 species of mostly viny perennial legumes native primarily in tropical and warm temperate parts of Africa and Asia. The cultivated soybean, *Glyine max* (L.) Merrill, is the only member of the genus having an erect bushy plant with an annual growth habit. Not known in the wild state, it is thought to be derived, at least in part, from the viny North Asiatic species, *Glycine ussuriensis* Regel & Maack.

Soybeans first appeared as a cultivated crop in northern China about 3,000 years ago. Although apparently imported to North America at various times during the Colonial era and the early days of the Republic, they did not become a major crop in the U.S. much before World War II.

For human consumption, soybeans may be eaten either in the immature or mature stages of growth, or in various processed forms.

Adding a dry soybean product to small grain cereals substantially improves protein utilization over the components consumed individually.

Since fresh, immature soybeans are seldom found in either canned or frozen forms on supermarket shelves, they are an excellent vegetable for home gardeners, who may expect yields of 2 bushels of green pods per 100 feet or row. Soybeans have a relatively high protein content for a vegetable and are a good source of vitamin A.

Vegetable soybeans grow best where nights are warm and days not too long. Only very early varieties

Toasted soybeans make a tasty snack.

should be attempted at higher latitudes. They are unlikely to succeed in areas having frost-free growing seasons of less than 130 to 135 days.

Seeds of vegetable soybeans are usually larger than those grown as a field crop, and only a limited number of varieties, such as Fiskeby V and Kanrich, are offered currently by seedsmen. Most vegetable soybeans have yellow seeds, but other colors are known, such as green, black and green, and black and yellow.

Land on which edible soybeans are to be grown should be well prepared before planting. Soybeans do not thrive on strongly acid soils, and liming may be desirable if indicated by soil tests. Because they are legumes, nitrogenous fertilizers are seldom used, but on many soils they will benefit from application of phosphorus and potassium fertilizers (again the gardener should be guided by soil tests).

If soybeans have never been grown on the soil, it may prove wise to inoculate the seeds with nitrogen-fixing bacteria. *Rhizobium japonicum* is said to be specific for soybeans, and should be available in commercial preparations.

Weed control will be more convenient if the plants are spaced 4 to 6 inches apart, or in hills spaced about 8 inches apart with the rows 30 inches apart. When seeds of varieties differing in maturity are available, better results will ensue if a single planting of these is made—rather than successive plantings of a single variety.

Under favorable conditions, edible soybeans will be ready for harvest as immature beans from early varieties about 2 months after planting, while 100 or more days of favorable weather will be needed to mature dry beans.

Soybeans are self-fertile and have

241

mostly self-pollinated flowers. The beans are borne in pods that are produced in clusters of 3 to 15. The pods are slightly curved and hairy, and will average 2 to 3 seeds per pod. In the Orient, the immature pods and seed are eaten together, but this has seldom been done in the United States. When eaten in the immature stage, vegetable soybeans are harvested at about the same maturity as immature lima beans.

If vegetable soybeans are to be eaten as green beans, the pods will shell much easier if they are plunged into boiling water for about 2 minutes, after which the beans can be squeezed from the pods without any difficulty.

If dry mature soybeans are desired, the plants should be cut when the

Cabbage looper, a major vegetable pest, feeds on soybean leaf.

pods are turning brown and windrowed or placed on a rack under shelter until fully matured, when the seeds may be beaten out. This prevents loss through shattering in the garden. Following shelling, dry the seeds thoroughly before storage.

Another way of using edible soybeans is as sprouts (in the same manner as the sprouts of mung beans). Soybeans can be sprouted in any container that has holes in the bottom for drainage and can be covered.

In preparing the sprouts, soak the soybeans overnight and then place them in a container large enough for the beans to swell at least six times

Fred Farout

their original bulk as they sprout. Cover container to keep out light.

Moisten the beans at least 3 times a day in summer and twice in winter. In winter add warm water and keep the beans in a warm place.

Time to maturity for soybean sprouts is 3 to 5 days in summer and 10 to 15 days in winter. The sprouts are fully grown and ready to be used when 2 to 3 inches long. Once harvested, sprouts should be kept in a cool, humid place.

At least 25 parasitic diseases are common on soybeans in various parts of the United States, variously caused by bacteria, fungi and viruses. In most cases, the best defense is the planting of resistant varieties, or in the case of seed-borne viruses, of virus-free seeds.

In various parts of the United States, soybeans may be attacked by the green clover worm, the thistle caterpillar, the army worm, by leafhoppers, mites, grasshoppers and blister beetles.

Watercress

Watercress (*Rorippa nasturtium-aquaticm* [L.] Schinz & Thell.) is a popular cool-season salad vegetable. Like collards, broccoli, turnips and their relatives, watercress is a member of the Mustard Family (Cruciferae or Brassicaceae). The generic name is thought to be derived from *rorippen,* the ancient Saxon common name for watercress. This perennial plant has its natural distribution in Europe and western Asia, but has become naturalized extensively throughout the cool-temperate climatic areas of the world.

Portions of the plant commonly eaten are the upper 4 to 6 inches of the vegetative stems and associated leaves. Watercress gives a pungent flavor to salads, makes a novelty sandwich filling, is sometimes used as a flavoring in soups, and serves as an attractive garnish.

Watercress grows naturally in clear, cold, shallow, slow-moving creeks. It may grow either as a floating plant, become rooted in the bottom, or creep along wet stream margins.

Watercress grows well on rich, slightly acid to slightly alkaline garden soils (pH not lower than 6.0), for which ample irrigation is available. Plantings can be established readily by means of stem cuttings, or by raising plants from seeds.

Home gardeners may adopt either the trench or surface culture systems for watercress.

For those particularly fond of high quality watercress, the trench system of culture may be well worth the effort involved. In this system a trench is dug 2 feet deep and 2 to 3 feet wide. A 9-inch layer of well-rotted compost or manure is placed in the bottom of the trench and allowed to settle for about 2 weeks. Irrigate daily at the rate of 3 to 4 gallons of water per yard of trench length. At the end of the period, put 4 inches of good topsoil over the organic mass and press it down firmly.

The prepared trench may be planted either with seeds or stem cuttings. If seeds are used, the gardener will find them to be quite small—about 150,000 per ounce—and to have a rather low germination standard, about 40% to 50%. The trench should be marked off in a grid of 8-inch squares, and several seeds planted at each intersection in the grid.

Cover the seeds with about 1/16th inch of fine sand. Mist the planting frequently, so that it never dries out, and keep the trench dark by covering with some material that will exclude light, laid over a supporting framework.

After germination is complete, remove the opaque covering and thin the seedlings to 1 per intersection. Give the trench a good flooding after thinning.

If stem cuttings are to be used as

planting stock, they may be collected from the wild. Or bunched watercress from the supermarket may be used. Plant one cutting at each intersection on the 8 x 8 inch grid, and water thoroughly.

With either starting method, keep the soil free from weeds by hand weeding until the watercress plants grow large enough to provide strong competition for them. Never allow the soil to dry out. The plants will benefit from being irrigated daily with a fine mist nozzle, except in rainy weather.

As soon as the plants have reached about 6 inches in height, pinch the leading shoot to encourage branching. The plants should not be permitted to flower. As soon as signs of flower buds are observed, cut the plants back.

It takes 60 to 70 days for watercress to reach harvest maturity from seeds, somewhat less from cuttings. Hence, in mild climatic areas it may be a good plan to start a succession of trench cultures about a month apart to assure continuity of quality harvests.

In the surface culture system, prepare the soil with a high level of organic matter from manure or compost. A bed of several short rows will be easier to handle than a single long row. Rows in the bed may be placed 12 to 18 inches apart. Sow the seeds very shallowly at the rate of 0.5 ounce per 100 feet of row. Even distribution of the seeds will be readily achieved if they are first mixed with a very fine-textured dry sand.

The planting should be kept wet throughout germination, emergence, and seedling establishment. As soon as the first true leaves appear, the seedlings may be thinned to stand 8 to 10 inches apart in the row. Maintain constantly high soil moisture levels for best results.

An alternative to direct seeding in the garden is starting the seed in small peat pots under a mist propagation system, provided you have a greenhouse equipped for this. Sow several seeds in each pot, thinning to one seedling after the first true leaves have appeared.

Well-started seedlings may be transplanted to the prepared bed in the garden, pot and all, or possibly maintained under mist in the greenhouse for nearly year-around harvest. Due to leaching effects of the mist, occasional application of liquid fertilizer is advised to maintain vigorous growth.

Apart from the above, cultural practices for surface culture are similar to those for the trench system.

In harvesting watercress, take a sharp knife and cut about 6 inches of the leading shoots or side shoots. Tie the cut pieces into bunches and trim the butt ends so the finished bunch is about 4 inches long. The harvested bunches may be kept in water, or possibly in plastic wrapping in the refrigerator for limited periods. The home gardener can expect to harvest one bunch of watercress per foot of row.

Watercress in the United States has not been found to be damaged seriously by diseases. Aphids, leaf beetles, leafhoppers and sowbugs sometimes attack watercress. For currently recommended control measures, consult your county Extension agent.

244